THE GAME ANGLER IN IRELAND

BY KEN WHELAN

FOREWORD BY JACK CHARLTON

COUNTRY HOUSE

Published by
Country House
41 Marlborough Road
Donnybrook
Dublin 4
Ireland

First published in 1989 as part of
The Angler in Ireland: Game, Coarse & Sea.

This edition published in 1991.
© Ken Whelan 1989, 1991

All rights reserved. No part of this publication may be reproduced, stored in a retrieval system, or transmitted in any form or by any means, electronic, mechanical, photocopying, recording or otherwise, without the prior permission of the publishers.

British Library Cataloguing in Publication Data
Whelan, Ken *1951-*
    The game angler in Ireland.
    1. Ireland. Angling
    I. Title
    799.1209415

ISBN 0-946172-22-6

Managing editor: Treasa Coady
Illustrator and designer: Bill Murphy
Photography: Mike Bunn
Text editors: Elaine Campion, Siobhán Parkinson
Typeset by Printset & Design Ltd, Dublin
Colour separation by Kulor Centre, Dublin
Printed in Hong Kong

CONTENTS

List of colour photographs

List of black and white photographs

ACKNOWLEDGEMENTS

To acknowledge all of those who contributed to this book would be an almost impossible task; for angling books are never really original works, they are a distillation of experiences, thoughts, conversations and views. To attribute to each friend or acquaintance their rightful credit is patently impossible. All I can do is to thank those who have contributed directly to the production of the final work and to collectively acknowledge my gratitude to the many other anglers and friends who have influenced my thinking on angling over the years.

First and foremost I must thank 'the team' who contributed generously and enthusiastically to the book and its creation: Treasa Coady, my publisher; Bill Murphy, illustrator and designer; Mike Bunn, photographer; Elaine Campion and Siobhán Parkinson, copy editors; and to Phil Browne who did such an excellent job in typing and formatting the original text.

To the many people who provided original technical material for inclusion in the book, and to all of those who took so much trouble in facilitating photographic sessions, particularly those whose patience was sorely tried by the vagaries of the weather and the photographer's craft. The manuscript was read and objectively criticised by a range of specialists, whose incisive comments have greatly improved the technical precision of the text; none the less, any remaining errors or omissions are my own.

I am grateful to the following for permission to use passages from their publications: The Central Fisheries Board; Bord Fáilte; Herbert Jenkins.

A special word of thanks must go to my parents and family, especially my father and my brother Brendan, constant angling companions for over thirty years, who have helped to make so many angling dreams come true. Their patience, interest and active support in all of my 'mad cap' schemes is rarely articulated but much appreciated.

Finally and most importantly, to my dear wife Frances, for all of the sacrifices she has made to ensure the completion of the book, particularly her patience and ingenuity in keeping the family amused while I scribbled away incessantly for almost a year; to my children David and Laura without whom the text would have been completed in half the time but whose very existence has made the whole project so worthwhile.

Ken Whelan
Newport, Co. Mayo
March 1991

FOREWORD

One of the many perks which came with my job as manager of the Irish soccer team was the opportunity to sample the range and quality of angling available in Ireland. And what splendid fishing there is – the spring salmon of the big rivers, the lively grilse and sea trout of the summer, the teeming brown trout in all parts of the country. I could go on and on. Most of all, compared to the crowded British and continental waters, the anglers are few and far between. I enjoy fishing in Ireland, and I know a lot of anglers who are only now discovering Ireland as an angling destination.

Now, at last, there is a comprehensive book on all forms of game angling in Ireland. This is not just a guide to Irish angling or a 'how-to-do-it' manual, it is a great read for anglers anywhere. Ken combines his passion for angling with his training as a scientist. The result is that rare combination – a scientist who can communicate the latest knowledge about fish and fishing in a fascinating and readable way. I love to learn about the behaviour and habits of my quarry and I found this aspect of the book particularly absorbing. It is in no way a dry or difficult text and the photography is great. It combines biological insights with sound advice on tackle and descriptions of methods and locations, with many amusing stories and scenes culled from a lifetime of fish chasing.

This book will be read with pleasure and profit by anglers everywhere, but those visiting Ireland from abroad will particularly benefit from it. The specialist will appreciate the detailed advice on locations, tackle and local methods while the beginner will find the author's sound common sense an invaluable guide in his early efforts. I hope the book will encourage visitors to 'have a go' and fish for species that they do not usually catch at home. Such angling opportunities abound in Ireland and are within easy reach of every major angling centre.

I can heartily recommend this book – I hope other anglers can get from it some of the benefit and pleasure it has given me.

Jack Charlton
Dalton, March 1991

INTRODUCTION

Until relatively recently, going fishing in Ireland meant going trout fishing. Trout and their migratory cousins the white or sea trout abounded in every stream, river, lake and pond. There was hardly a community in Ireland which did not have access to some form of trout fishing.

Not so with the lordly salmon. He was the domain of the landed gentry, the landlord's fish, a creature of rare strength and beauty, but even more importantly of high commercial value. Rights to the premier salmon fisheries were jealously guarded and, unless one was fortunate enough to be in the employ of the local estate, it was doubtful if the chance to angle for this powerful adversary would ever come your way.

At the turn of this century Ireland was, in fish terms, similar to the Alaska of today. It had largely escaped the ravages of the industrial revolution and fish abounded in its pollution-free lakes, rivers and streams, and in its totally unexploited seas.

Rod catches of trout were measured by the dozen and seasonal salmon catches in thousands of pounds. One example will suffice to illustrate this point. An angler fishing on the lower River Suir from 1 February to 15 June 1928 caught sixty-nine salmon. Nothing extraordinary in that you might add. However, the fish weighed 1487lb (675kg); the best fish was 45½lb (21kg) and the smallest 6lb (2.5kg). His average weight for the season was 21½lb (10kg). Similar statistics are available from other mighty rivers such as the Nore, Munster Blackwater, Shannon and Moy.

The visiting angler

In order to be successful, it is very important that visiting anglers have a real appreciation of the present state of angling in Ireland. It is true that, comparatively speaking, Ireland has arguably the finest variety of angling available anywhere in Europe. It can still boast great lake fisheries which are as yet uncharted and some of the finest wild brown trout fishing to be found anywhere in the world.

However, like many other developing countries, Ireland's fisheries have suffered at the hands of so-called industrial and agricultural progress. The problems facing Irish angling must be contrasted with the vast resource which remains unscathed by modern-day advances. Ireland is a sparsely populated country with the majority of its people centred either along its Eastern coastline or in large urban centres.

Using this book

If the angler is to be successful on his first visit to Ireland he must do two things: he must carefully choose the water or waters to be fished and have a comprehensive knowledge of his quarry and the most up-to-date methods used in its capture.

The main purpose of this book is to provide the angler with a comprehensive review of the species which he is likely to encounter while fishing in Ireland, to give some biological facts on the various species and to list the modern methods of capturing each species or group of fish.

I firmly believe that the more successful angler is the one who appreciates the basic behavioural biology of his quarry and can make intelligent decisions regarding the reaction of his quarry to various environmental conditions.

It is obviously not possible to include in one volume all of the specialist information which is available on any given species. The reader will, however, be referred to other articles and books containing such material, should he wish to expand his knowledge of any one species of fish.

The book is intended for those who have a basic knowledge of angling and no effort is made to give instructions on basic techniques such as casting. Therefore, it is assumed that if one decides to go fly fishing for salmon in spring, the rudiments of assembling the tackle and casting a double-handed rod are known. If this is not the case, the reader is advised to obtain tuition from one of the many excellent casting schools which are run, at various locations, throughout the summer months.

Measurements are given in both their imperial and metric forms, except in the case of metres and kilometres where only the metric form is used. The metric conversions are intended only as a guide and are generally rounded to the nearest half unit.

In general there is a great deal of nonsense talked about the 'proper' tackle and the limitations of using a general set of all-purpose equipment. When one considers that the fish generally sees, at most, no more than 1 to 3ft (30–90cm) of the cast or leader, it matters little to him what type of rod, reel or indeed angler is attached to the other end of the equipment.

Most visiting anglers will come equipped with at least one 8–9ft (2.5m) all-purpose fibreglass or carbon fibre spinning rod and matching spinning reel. If they also possess a standard 9ft (2.5m) glass or carbon fly rod and two fly lines, a floating line and a medium-sinking line, they have the basic capability to tackle all of the species described in this book. The visitor will find that to possess such basic equipment will raise him above the status of a mere tourist to the exalted position of tourist angler. He will suddenly find that he is a fellow member of an international confraternity where even language is no barrier to communication.

Although I have attempted to lighten each chapter through the inclusion of anecdotes and fishermen's stories, my book remains above all a fishing manual. The readers will notice that, throughout the text, fish are referred to as 'he' rather than 'it'. This is a standard convention in angling writing; the pronoun is used in an asexual sense to personalise the relationship between the angler and the fish. Its use is not intended, in any way, to degrade or denigrate the female of the species.

It is my earnest hope that the readers will benefit over time from this book; that their bags will increase in both weight and variety as a result, and that it will encourage them to experiment with new species and new fishing environments so that they too can gain even a fraction of the enjoyment which Irish angling has given me over the past thirty years.

Licence requirements

Anglers are advised to check with the relevant authorities regarding the up-to-date position on licences and permits before commencing fishing. A list of the principal state agencies involved is provided in Appendix 2.

In recent years sea trout catches in Connemara and south Mayo have been particularly poor. Anglers are advised to check with the appropriate Regional Fisheries Board (see Appendix 2) before booking a sea trout holiday in these areas.

NOTE: On occasions throughout this book, cross-references are made. The page numbers given refer to the original edition, that is, The Angler in Ireland: Game, Coarse & Sea **(Country House, 1989). Such references should be ignored.**

CHAPTER 1

THE FRESHWATER RESOURCE

Underlying geology

Ireland's natural freshwater resources are truly immense. Compressed into a total land area of just 84 000km² are 16 000km of main river channels, at least a further 10 000km of tributary streams and over 500 000 acres (200 000 ha) of lakes; roughly one-fortieth of the country's total area.

Like its politics, the geology of Ireland is highly complex, with strange and exotic strata appearing amongst otherwise homogeneous rock. The underlying geology directly affects the productivity of the waters, and of course their ability to produce large harvests of fish. Ireland can be looked on as a dog-shaped saucer with a central oval plain of soft carboniferous limestone and outer margins of progressively harder rock. The immediate edges of the limestone plain are etched with the softer sandstones, while the coastline is generally bordered by harder granite-type rocks.

When describing the alkalinity or degree of hardness of the water, it is useful to refer to what is called the pH of the water. In natural waters this parameter normally varies between values of 4 and 8. A pH of 7 is considered neutral — neither acidic nor alkaline. Because it is a logarithmic scale, each unit on the scale represents a tenfold increase or decrease away from neutrality. Therefore, a pH of, say, 8, is ten times more alkaline than neutrality (pH7) and pH5 is one hundred times more acidic. The rich limestone waters of the central plain display pH values of 8 or more, while the sandstones lie between 6 and 7. Some of the waters flowing off the Wicklow or Connemara mountains may have natural pH values below 5.

It has been known for many years that the relative productivity of the various waters in Ireland is directly related to their alkalinity. For this reason the best brown trout fishing, in terms of the average size of the fish, and the best coarse fishing are to be found in the alkaline limestone areas, while the acid sandstone and granite areas generally produce moderate to poor brown trout angling but excellent salmon and sea trout angling. In the acid areas nature has adapted extraordinarily well to the low productivity of the systems and has more than compensated for low individual growth rates. Exceptionally large numbers of salmonid fry and parr are produced, which feed only sparingly in fresh water but which, once they have migrated to the sea, make full use of the ocean's rich feeding.

From time to time the angler may, however, come upon pleasant geological anomalies; limestone intrusions may appear in the most unlikely places. Some years ago I was involved in a survey of lakes and river systems in north Donegal. After spending several weeks assessing the various waters, we had, I must admit, become rather complacent regarding the small size of the trout which we would encounter. One evening in late July we arrived at the shore of a small mountain lake and duly set about the task of assembling our survey nets. While doing so we chanced to meet a local farmer who claimed to have fished the lake for many years. Yes, there were fish in the lake and indeed it had been stocked at one stage, and he himself had seen them taken on the dry fly up to 7lb (3kg) in weight, but very few fish had been caught. When he had departed the scene we discussed this information, but given the bleak, barren landscape which lay before us we decided to discount his claims. Imagine our surprise and embarrassment the following morning when we discovered thirty trout in our survey nets, fifteen of which were between 5 and 8lb (2.5–3.5kg) in weight. Luckily the majority of these fish were merely tangled in our small-meshed nets and they were released back into the lake unharmed.

On further examination, we found that the lake lay in a limestone depression and held large quantities of both freshwater snails and newts. Because of very poor spawning facilities, the lake held few, if any, natural trout. When stocked, however, the trout grew exceptionally fast, with some reaching 10lb (4.5kg) in a matter of eight years.

Freshwater species

There is still a great deal of uncertainty regarding which species of freshwater fish were introduced into Ireland and which occurred naturally. A total of thirty-four species has been recorded from fresh water in Ireland. Of these, eight are predominantly marine and are only occasional visitors to fresh water. A further fourteen species are thought to have been introduced. This leaves a possible total of twelve indigenous fish species. The Irish freshwater fish fauna is therefore limited compared with that of Britain, where fifty-five species have been recorded. Britain's fauna is, in turn, poor compared with that of continental Europe, where some one hundred and thirty different fish species exist.

Since many of the non-salmonid species of freshwater fish (cyprinids, pike, perch, etc) have a low tolerance for salt water, it follows that post-glacial colonisation must have taken place through river systems flowing over land-bridges. The land-bridge linking southern Britain with mainland Europe is known to geologists as Doggerland. Before this area was submerged by rising seas, the Thames was a tributary of the Rhine which flowed across Doggerland into the restricted North Sea. Many coarse fish species invaded Britain through this route before the land-bridge disappeared — about 9000 years ago. As the great ice sheets melted, the sea levels began to rise and the land-bridge between Ireland and Scotland was flooded and quickly disappeared. The newly formed rivers were slowly colonised by anadromous salmonids such as the char, trout and salmon. The barren, gravel-laden rivers probably attracted the salmonids as ideal spawning areas which also provided a safe haven for their young.

As conditions stabilised in the newly formed freshwater catchments and stable food chains developed, subgroups of these early salmonids lost their migratory instinct and established resident populations. Irish trout and char stocks are now largely represented by resident stocks, although sea trout, or even sea run brown trout, do occur in most small coastal streams and in maritime lake systems about the coast.

Coarse fish is a term normally reserved for pike and perch and the cyprinids. However, it also includes such species as the eel, minnow, stoneloach and gudgeon. Documentary evidence exists to show that at least seven species were introduced into Ireland within the last 400 years or so. The Irish (Gaelic) name for the most ubiquitous of these exotic species, the pike, is *gaill-iasc*, which literally means foreign fish or the foreigner's fish, and there is no name for pike in the old Irish language.

The first documented evidence for the importation of tench and carp was in 1634. However, monastic settlements probably imported carp from Britain and Europe long before this date. Both species require high summer temperatures to spawn, and self-sustaining populations were only established in isolated areas. However, they are highly prized by anglers. Throughout the 1950s and the 1960s the Inland Fisheries Trust carried out successful stocking of both carp and tench on carefully selected waters. The programme was highly successful and stocks of large tench, in particular, are now a feature of many midland and east coast coarse fisheries.

Roach and dace were unknown in Ireland before 1889 when they were accidently introduced into the Munster Blackwater by a British pike angler. Both this occurrence and a further introduction into the Fairywater, County Tyrone, are well authenticated. However, since 1968, populations of roach have established themselves in many large catchments throughout the country. They are now firmly established in the Erne, Shannon, Corrib, Boyne and Liffey catchments.

Cyprinid species also hybridise readily and the presence in a fishery of good stocks of rudd/bream or roach/bream hybrids may act as a key attraction to visiting coarse anglers. In contrast to most hybrid animals, cyprinid hybrids are fertile. They may average 4lb (2kg) or more at spawning time, when they are most accessible to the lake shore angler.

Fish in plenty

The visiting angler may not find in Ireland the diversity of species for which other countries are justly famous. He will, however, discover that many of Ireland's waters, both game and coarse, hold an abundance of fish of a large average size. He will also discover that, due to Ireland's low density of population, many of the better waters are little fished, except at peak angling times. Some brief examples may serve to illustrate this point.

A recent survey of the River Suir (Counties Tipperary and Waterford) has shown that there are almost 400km of good to excellent brown trout waters in the main river and its tributaries and that it could accommodate, at a conservative estimate, 1000 anglers at any given time. At present, apart from well known stretches of the main channel, the visiting angler would be fortunate to meet another angler.

Lough Ree (County Roscommon) is an immense sheet of water, some 26 000 acres (10 500ha) in extent; however, access is limited to some twelve locations around the lake shore. It is one of the principal lakes of the mighty River Shannon and is home to vast untouched shoals of coarse and game fish. It is a high pH water in which the residents grow fast and achieve a large average size. It is one of the truly great mixed fisheries left in Ireland and when one is trolling, a 20lb (9kg) salmon, a 10 or 15lb (4.5-6.5kg) trout or even a 40lb (18kg) pike are real possibilities.

The River Moy, which flows into the sea near Ballina, County Mayo, is approximately 80km long and drains Lough Conn (14 000 acres; 5700ha), one of the best game fisheries in Ireland. It is itself one of the most productive salmon systems in Ireland, if not in Europe. Average yearly rod catches are between 3000 and 5000 salmon, and a further 10 000 or so fish are taken in the commercial fishery at Ballina. In contrast to the other two waters named, the Moy could certainly not be described as underfished nor, due to a very severe arterial drainage scheme carried out in the mid-fifties, could it be described as ideally suited to the fly. Fortunately, the drainage scheme had the effect of exposing vast quantities of alluvial gravels, which has resulted in the production of very large numbers of juvenile salmon. Commercial fishing in the lower Moy and some of the lower angling pools was taken into state ownership in 1987, and it is hoped, by a system of judicious management, to increase the rod catch on all beats over the next decade or so.

CHAPTER 2

SALMON

Anadromous life cycle

Life cycle and biology

The Atlantic salmon *(Salmo salar)* displays what biologists call an anadromous life cycle. That is to say, the young are born in fresh water but after a defined period they migrate to the sea to feed and grow. Because of this dual existence and the salmon's uncanny knack of locating its parent stream or river on its return from the sea, its life cycle has been the subject of many articles, papers and films.

Salmon eggs are deposited in gravel depressions, called redds, during the months of November and December. Water temperature regulates the rate at which they hatch but normally the redd is home to the fertilised salmon eggs for the following three to four months. The eggs become 'eyed' within six to eight weeks. After this the backbone appears and gradually the small fish takes shape. By mid to late March the eggs begin to hatch and yolk sac fry appear. These are small, transparent, brown creatures with protruding eyes and a yolk sac suspended from their bodies. Gradually the yolk sac is absorbed and salmon fry or alevins appear.

It is at this stage that the fry emerge from the gravel of the redd and begin to feed. After a few days they become territorial and compete for space. The larger fry take up station on or around the redd, while the weaker fry are dispersed downstream.

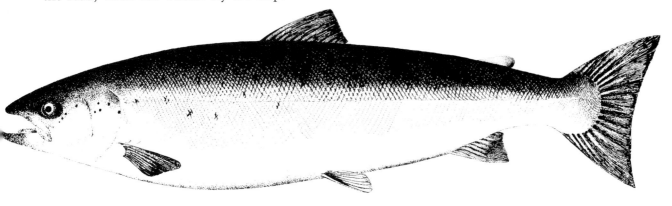

Young salmon are opportunistic feeders and consume a variety of organisms, ranging from tiny chironomid larvae living amongst the mosses to great earthworms, daddy-long-legs, beetles and caterpillars, carried down by spates or blown onto the stream by obliging winds. It has only recently become apparent just how important the terrestrial component of their diet is to the survival and growth of juvenile salmon, particularly in the poorer mountain streams. The salmon parr inhabit the faster water at the neck of pools and long shallow runs. The slower flowing pool areas are left to the resident brown trout.

The young salmon grow fast and by the end of their first summer may measure 3 to 4in (7.5–10cm). The larger parr, as they are now called, may migrate to the sea the following May, at one year old and at a length of 5in (13cm), but the majority of parr spend a further year in fresh water before migrating. In some catchments where food is particularly scarce, parr may remain for yet a further twelve months.

About six to eight weeks prior to migration the sleek parr begin to turn silvery. The spots and 'thumbprints' along their flanks disappear and eventually only those on the gill-covers remain. The juvenile salmon has now become a smolt. Physiologically the fish is undergoing tremendous changes, in preparation for its entry into salt water, and these changes force it to move downstream in search of an environment where it may once again regulate its salt and water balance.

From fresh to salt water

In fresh water the parr is engaged in a continuous struggle to retain its body salts and to avoid the retention of surplus water, while in salt water the smolt must guard against the loss of water and must be capable of secreting excess salt from its body fluids. This is what scientists call osmoregulation. It is only certain groups of fish which are capable of making the full transition from fresh to salt water.

Because smolts are under such extreme physiological stress when just about to leave fresh water, they must be handled with extreme care if mortalities are to be avoided. The jumping, flashing, silver salmon smolt, so frequently encountered by the angler during April and early May, is a creature undergoing the most extreme discomfort. The added stress of being hooked and released by the angler may just be enough to kill it if the greatest care is not taken in unhooking, handling and returning the fish to the water.

The migrations of these salmon smolts once they have reached the sea are legendary. However, in reality we have little detailed knowledge of their behaviour. We know that some remain to feed actively in neighbouring estuaries or bays for several weeks before migrating northwards. Still others move out to sea almost immediately after entering salt water.

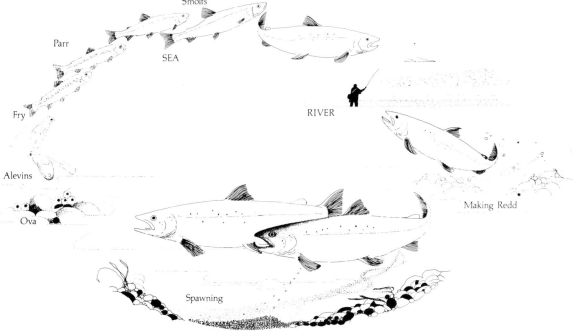

Life cycle of the salmon

Smolts

Parr

SEA

Fry

RIVER

Alevins

Ova

Making Redd

Spawning

The smolts move northwards into a great feeding area stretching from east of the Faroe Islands to west of Greenland. Here the salmon stay feeding for periods of one to four years. Salmon which return to fresh water after one year's feeding are known as grilse, and these average approximately 6lb (2.5kg) in weight. The remaining fish are known as salmon, or more correctly, multi-sea-winter stocks, and their size depends on the length of time they remain feeding at sea. The two-sea-winter fish normally return from January through to May and these range in weight from 10 to 20lb (4.5–9kg). The three-and four-sea-winter fish may weigh from 20 to 40lb (9–18kg) or more. Unfortunately, these older maiden stocks are now rare amongst Irish salmon.

While at sea, salmon feed on a variety of organisms including capelin, herring, small cod, pollack, sandeels, sprats and a variety of the larger shrimps and prawns which inhabit the rich fauna of the North Atlantic. When salmon feeding grounds were discovered off west Greenland in the mid to late sixties, and grilse feeding grounds were found south of the Faroes a decade later, it was assumed that the two main feeding areas for one-sea-winter and multi-sea-winter salmon had been discovered. However, it is now obvious that the pelagic salmon is a dynamic creature which follows the movements of its prey throughout the great expanse of the North Atlantic, and hard and fast rules regarding the location of its feeding grounds from year to year are difficult to apply.

The other great question which has taxed the minds of anglers, scientists and naturalists for centuries is how nature selects one group of salmon to stay at sea for a year or less while others remain for three or even four years. It is now apparent that there is a genetic component which regulates the production of multi-sea-winter stocks. This component may be masked by a series of as yet undefined environmental triggers. It is thought, for instance, that the cyclical dearth and abundance of alternating grilse and salmon stocks is regulated, at least in part, by the movements of cold and warm water currents throughout the North Atlantic. It seems that the choice of whether a smolt is destined to become a grilse or a salmon is made at sea.

Return to fresh water

Because of the overlapping components of the salmon stocks — grilse, previous spawners, spring, summer and autumn salmon — fresh salmon enter many of our larger fisheries every month of the year. However, significant runs appear at very definite times. The so-called spring salmon (two- and three-sea-winter fish in Ireland) enter the rivers between December and May, and the grilse enter from May to late July. In recent years there has been a distinct and very welcome run of late grilse in August and September. It is my own view that these are a transitory group which will eventually remain at sea until early winter and return as part of the two-sea-winter component. On their return to fresh water, both salmon and grilse cease to feed and display all the classic symptoms of a human anorexic. The physiological and biochemical changes are similar and salmon are presently being used as experimental animals in the study of this disorder. The fish live for periods of eight to fourteen months off the fats and proteins stored in their body musculature. Since most salmon fisheries have extremely poor feeding and can barely support their stocks of resident trout and juvenile salmon, nature has designed matters so that the returning adults put little or no pressure on these scarce food resources.

By autumn, male and female salmon are easily distinguishable. Both have lost the characteristic silver flanks. The male's nuptial coat is composed of appropriate seasonal colours — russet, brown, orange and red, all delicately blended into an overall copper sheen. The hook or kype on the lower jaw is his most distinguishing feature. The females are almost black, their bodies swollen and distended by developing eggs. To conserve their strength the fish lie in quiet eddies and resting places throughout October. They have encountered waterfalls, rapids and battled many miles upstream since leaving the sea in early summer. They are well aware of what lies before them.

Spawning

By mid-November the spawning urge has become almost overpowering, and first the males, then the females, begin their journey to the spawning beds. The homing instinct of the salmon is so finely tuned that fish will often spawn on or near the bank of gravel where they themselves were spawned. The number of eggs laid is directly related to size. A 6lb fish may lay 5000 eggs while a twenty-pounder could shed 15 000!

Spawning normally takes place during December. Experts differ as to what attracts the female salmon to the exact redd. But one thing they all agree on is that salmon have a knack of choosing the ideal location for their eggs.

For some days prior to spawning, the female may be seen moving around gravelly, fast-flowing areas of the stream. At times she flashes and uses her tail to dislodge stones and gravel. In this manner she tests the ground, looking for an area where the water flow through the gravel is strong and where her eggs will be well oxygenated and safe for their four-month incubation period.

The spawning act takes place around dusk. The female moves forward and, using flapping movements of her tail, she excavates a depression some six inches to one foot (15–30cm) deep in the gravel. When just about to spawn she rests her lower or anal fins against the bottom of the stream, as if to test the depth of the redd. The male has by this time joined her and carried out a series of shuddering, quivering body movements. As the male's stimulation reaches its peak the female extrudes a stream of orange eggs into the redd. Simultaneously the male releases a cloud of white milt which drifts downstream and covers the eggs.

Often at this point some small salmon parr may be seen to dart in and release sperm into the redd. These are precocious male parr which mature at only one year of age. (Up to 75 per cent of male salmon parr mature in their second year.) These fish serve a useful role for they inject the milt deep into the redd, ensuring maximum fertilisation.

After spawning, the male leaves the female to cover the eggs with the disturbed gravel and stones. He moves off to rest and spawn again with other ripe females.

Once spawned, Atlantic salmon are known as kelts. Some die immediately after spawning but the survivors return to the sea. They can make their descent at any time between December and March but generally they return in two groups. The first migrates immediately after spawning. The remaining fish rest until February or March in the quiet pools and eddies, recovering from the rigours of spawning. They gradually develop a silver sheen and regain some of their former vigour, though they are characterised by large heads and a terrible thinness about the body. Some 30 to 50 per cent of the spawning adults live to reach the ocean, and on average only three out of every twenty are males. Weakened by spawning and their year-long fast, many of these fish fall prey to predators, and only about 5 per cent return to spawn a second time.

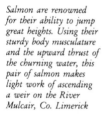

Salmon are renowned for their ability to jump great heights. Using their sturdy body musculature and the upward thrust of the churning water, this pair of salmon makes light work of ascending a weir on the River Mulcair, Co. Limerick

Survival rates

Throughout its long wandering life cycle, the salmon is exposed to many dangers and natural enemies. At different life stages the principal predators of salmon are herons, mergansers, gulls, cormorants, trout, pike, pollack, bass, cod, shark and seals. Less than one out of every 100 eggs may ultimately become a smolt, but in a good year as many as forty out of every 100 smolts may survive to return to the coast as adults. Why is it then that such high sea-survival rates do not result in an abundance of salmon entering our rivers? The reason is simple. Amongst all of his enemies, people pose the greatest threat to the survival and well-being of the salmon.

Stocks and management

Freshwater escapement

In salmon fishing, angling success is directly related to freshwater escapement, which in turn is largely controlled by the efficiency of the commercial fisheries. Over the last twenty years there has been a complete reversal in the efficiency and use of offshore gill nets in Ireland. Traditionally, some 50 per cent or more of the annual salmon catch was taken in draft nets, fished in estuaries or bays. The remainder of the catch was taken by drift nets, snap nets, bag nets, crib fisheries and by angling, which generally accounted for 10 to 15 per cent of the total. However, since the early seventies, the drift nets have continued to take an increasing share of the national catch and now account for more than 80 per cent. The percentage accruing to the other fisheries has dwindled and the anglers' take is down to 4 or 5 per cent.

Fortunately, some fisheries have survived the onslaught of the drift nets quite well, particularly the larger catchments in the west and north-west. Approximately ten fisheries now account for the bulk of the 30 000 or so salmon taken by rod and line each season. Angling statistics in Ireland, as in other countries, are generally an underestimate of the true situation. For instance, recent work on the River Moy has shown that only some 50 per cent of the annual catch is officially recorded by anglers.

The effects of UDN

During the mid-sixties, multi-sea-winter salmon stocks were hit by a mysterious and devastating disease. It was given the name ulcerative dermal necrosis, or UDN for short, and was characterised initially by the appearance of small bleached areas on the head, back and tail. As these patches spread, they became ulcerated and infected by fungus. It was most virulent at low temperatures and caused heavy mortalities amongst spring salmon and spawning stocks. Larger trout were also subject to the disease. Unfortunately the causative organism has never been isolated but it was almost certainly a virus.

Due to the ravages of UDN, salmon stocks declined quite dramatically for a period of ten to fifteen seasons. However, there are signs of a distinct recovery, and waters such as the Rivers Slaney, Munster Blackwater, Corrib, Drowse and Loughs Currane and Beltra now provide good fishing for spring salmon.

A recreational resource

Much has been written in recent years regarding the rational management of Ireland's wild salmon stocks, but sadly little has been done to curtail the illegal drift net fishing and to implement the fisheries laws. There is, however, a growing realisation of the value of our salmon stocks as a recreational resource.

Another factor working to the advantage of recreational salmon fishing is the unprecedented growth of salmon farming in Ireland. In less than a decade this industry has grown from a total production of 100 tonnes to more than 5000 tonnes, and it is confidently predicted that it will reach 11 000 tonnes, or close to five and a half million individual salmon, by 1992. The price of salmon has already dropped in real terms and there is little prospect that it will show any real increase for many years to come. This fact has serious implications for commercial wild salmon fisheries. Faced with dwindling prices, the ever more costly harvest of wild salmon may become less and less attractive to the larger trawlers.

Marketing

When selecting a fishery, the salmon angler is often perplexed by the array of facts and figures provided by the various proprietors. Generally, salmon angling is marketed on the previous year's total catch and advertisements in angling magazines will make such claims as '*600 salmon taken last season*' or '*our beats have averaged 1000 salmon over the past ten years*'. In addition, the best catch of the season is likely to be highlighted, '*Bill Sykes and partner had 8 grilse and 2 salmon in just five hours' fishing in September.*' It may be another fifty years before Bill and his friend repeat this performance but subconsciously each angler reading the advertisement sees himself replacing Bill during the next season.

The problem with all these accurate but misleading claims is that the all-important effort factor is not included. For instance, 500 salmon caught in 500 rod days is a very different matter to 500 salmon taken in 5000 rod days. More enlightened fishery managers are now including the blank days in their calculations and are relying on a statistic called catch per unit effort, or CPUE for short. What CPUE tells us is how many salmon per day are taken by an angler, on the fishery in question. Surprisingly, even in the best spate fisheries, the CPUE varies between 0.2 and 0.5. That is to say, it takes on average between two and five days' fishing to catch a salmon. Some exceptional fisheries, such as the lower pools on the Rivers Corrib and Moy may record a seasonal CPUE of between 1 and 2, but above such holding areas, within the main catchments, catch rates quickly revert to spate river levels.

When you take into account the Bill Sykeses of this world, who in one lucky day may take twenty people's share of the catch, it becomes obvious that there are a lot of blank days ahead of you during your salmon fishing career. To give any salmon fishery a fair chance, you should spend a minimum of three to five days fishing. If possible, bring along several companions, for sharing experiences in relation to various beats may make all the difference between success and failure.

Spring salmon fishing

Fishing for spring salmon is generally concentrated into the period mid-February to mid-May, although some fisheries open as early as 1 January (eg Rivers Liffey and Drowse). Spring salmon range in size from 8 to 16lb (3.5-7kg), but larger fish of 20lb (9kg) or more are not uncommon in some waters. Water temperatures in early spring can be as low as 1°C and cold-blooded salmon react accordingly. Unlike the grilse, early season salmon are less inclined to jump or splash on the surface. They hold station on the bottom and only slowly move upstream. As the water temperatures increase, the spring fish become more lively and at about 5°C they will jump barriers and cascades. It is not until water temperatures are above 10°C, however, that the salmon will consistently take a fly fished on a floating line.

Salmon lies
Spring salmon will continue to move slowly upstream even in relatively high and coloured water. Because of their tendency to lie close to the bottom, the angler must endeavour to keep his lure or fly well down in the water. Ideally the bait should be drawn past the salmon's nose, so that he has little to do except grab it and take it back into his lie. A knowledge of salmon lies, which consistently hold salmon year after year, can greatly enhance an angler's chance of taking a salmon.

This fact really came home to me some years ago while fishing below Ballycarney Bridge on the River Slaney. It was my first day on the water and the river was in high flood. About five o'clock in the evening I met a local angler who assured me that the area I was fishing did hold fish and he was kind enough to point out a few well-known lies. One of these was a very small eddy, perhaps a half metre by one and a half metres on the very far side of the swollen river. He assured me that running salmon often lingered in the eddy but were normally taken from the far bank. Since I was restricted to my own bank, I had no option but to put on a slightly larger three-inch Yellow Belly and cast across as far as possible. As I cast, the wind caught my lure and deposited it, not in the eddy but in the ploughed field beyond. I gently twitched back the lure across the broken bare earth, and to my amazement I managed to slip it into the water at the upper edge of the eddy. Almost immediately the line went completely taut. I cursed, for I was sure that the lure was snagged. Without thinking, I lifted the rod and in disgust yanked hard. In response, the line streaked out into the current. Seconds later a salmon of some 14lb (6kg) or more broke the surface. After two more sizzling runs the hook-hold gave and the salmon regained his freedom. I still wonder to this day what would have happened had I merely tightened into the fish.

The trout angler will find it difficult at first to come to terms with the salmon's rather odd preferences for certain quite extraordinary lies. One classic example is just above a very fast run. The fish hold in the gulley immediately above the flow, where the current is very strong. Fishing this type of lie can be very exciting, for all one has to do is cast the lure across the river from a position some 30 or 40m upstream and let the current take the bait across the lie. When the fish takes, he either bolts upstream into the pool or turns tail and heads back to sea. Thankfully he usually goes upstream, but if you should be unfortunate enough to have a large salmon turn tail into a strong current, you need both the grace of God and plenty of backing to land him!

Behavioural patterns

Since salmon are not feeding when they enter fresh water, why then do they take any interest in our flies and lures? Falkus, in his excellent book *Salmon Fishing*, discusses this topic at some length and concludes that in any given group of salmon there will be fish which will not have been entirely switched off from feeding and that some of their natural feeding or predatory responses may remain wholly or partially active. It is these fish we are most likely to tempt with our lures. He describes six types of take and the behaviour responsible for these. He names the six relevant behavioural patterns as: 'Feeding habit — strong, aggression, inducement, curiosity, irritation, playfulness.' In my experience these terms describe very accurately the actions which the angler will encounter in his prey when salmon fishing. I should add that, while a feeding or an aggressive take invariably results in a well-hooked fish, a series of playful or curious takes only leads to a dramatic rise in the angler's blood pressure!

EQUIPMENT

Fly rods

Spring salmon fishing with the fly requires the use of a 14-17ft (4-5m) double-handed fly rod. The tackle may be called on to handle anything from a size 4 double to a large 3-4in (7.5-10cm) brass tube fly. Line densities will also vary depending on conditions and a range of lines from AFTM 9 to 12 may be required. For these reasons, a salmon fly rod should be both resilient and light; modern carbon fibre has proved the ideal material.

Obviously no one fly rod will be suitable for all river types but by careful selection the angler may choose a single rod which will serve him well under most conditions. Take extra care, however, not to overtax your general purpose rod as this is easily done when punching out heavy tube flies into a strong wind. Before purchasing any rod the angler should field test it, if necessary in the company of an experienced friend. This is particularly true of double-handed salmon fly rods, for I have found them to be very variable in quality; the cheaper ones often lack the backbone to handle a long line satisfactorily.

Spinning rods

When spinning for spring salmon a 9-11ft (2.5-3.5m) carbon fibre or fibreglass double-handed rod is used. It should display a full action, that is to say, any strain should be spread evenly throughout the rod and not concentrated into the upper section or the rod tip. The rod should be both strong and rugged, for it may be called upon to handle large fish under the most extreme conditions of high water and wind. The baits used are often large and frequently require the addition of heavy leads if they are to fish effectively. Spinning in spring can be a slow, tedious business, and if the angler is to avoid the discomfort of an aching back or shoulder it is important to choose a rod which is reasonably light for its strength.

Fly reels

Salmon fly reels vary in diameter from 3½-4½in (9-11cm). The reel should be capable of holding the required fly line plus 100 to 150m of strong, 20-30lb (9-13.5kg) braided nylon backing. Ideally, the reel should be of good quality, light weight, with a dependable ratchet and drag system. To incorporate modern plastic-coated lines, the wide spool versions of the various reel designs are often required.

Spinning reels

The basic prerequisite of a spinning reel for spring salmon fishing is that it is capable of holding some 150 to 200m of 15-20lb (6.5-9kg) monofilament. The drag or tension control must be easily accessible and dependable but the choice between fixed spool or multiplier is one of individual preference. In the rivers which I fish I have found that the multiplier has certain disadvantages. It has a tendency to overrun, particularly when the angler is casting for distance. It also requires a heavy bait (1oz; 28g or more) and the use of a double-handed rod to achieve anything like the full potential casting distance of the reel.

Fly lines

Modern fly lines come in a wide variety of densities and designs. Spring salmon fishing may require the use of anything from a high-density shooting head to a standard double-tapered floating line. However, most fly fishing in spring is carried out using a medium to fast-rated sinking line or a sink-tip. The object of the exercise in spring is to ensure that the fly is well sunk as it passes through the salmon's lie. A good knowledge of the lies in a particular river, under varying water conditions, will prove a great advantage in choosing the correct density line for a given situation.

Landing nets and tailers

Landing your salmon may require the use of either

23

a landing net or a tailer. A large diameter 24–30in (60–80cm), long-handled 3–3½ft (1m) net is the ideal tool, but this requires the assistance of a colleague, particularly when dealing with really heavy fish. A tailer is more convenient for spring salmon and may be used by the lone angler. However, it is not as easy to use as it might seem and some practice is required before one becomes truly adept with the instrument. Two of the most common faults are inserting the tailer too high on the salmon's body (the noose should be kept well behind the dorsal fin), and attempting to tail the fish before he is fully played out. The use of a tailer is also suspect on salmon below around 7lb (3kg) as the wrist may be too narrow to accommodate the tailer. For grilse and small spring salmon the angler should either net or beach his prize.

Leaders (casts)

A dropper is rarely attached when spring salmon fishing. A 1m butt piece of nylon attached to 6–9ft (2–2.5m) of leader is adequate. Strengths vary depending on conditions but a butt piece of 20–30lb (9–13.5kg) and a 15–18lb (6.5–8kg) leader would normally be used.

TUCKED HALF-BLOOD KNOT

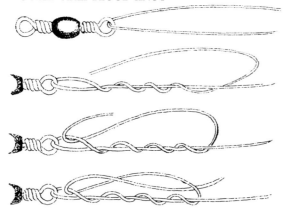

LOOP TO LOOP KNOT

UNIVERSAL KNOT

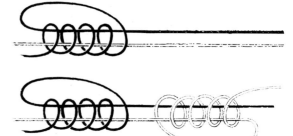

WHIPPING KNOT (SPADE END)

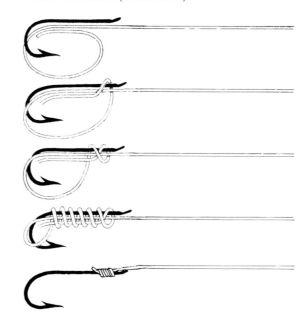

Three generations of beautifully patterned brown trout — an adult, a parr and a fry

Despite his bright fresh silvery coat, this salmon kelt is thin and emaciated (Photo courtesy CFB)

TECHNIQUES OF SPRING SALMON FISHING

It is a typical March morning with a heavy overcast sky, a moderate north-west breeze and a sharp nip in the air; last night's temperatures dropped to −2°C and so it will take most of the morning for the air temperatures to recover.

Dave and I have been invited to fish a stretch of the River Slaney in County Wexford. On our way across Ballycarney Bridge we noted that the river was running both high and coloured, so I have chosen a 3in (7.5cm) yellow belly Devon to start with. I will fish the bait on a 10ft (3m) double-handed, carbon fibre spinning rod and a fixed-spool reel loaded with 200m of 18lb (8kg) monofilament. If the water fines down during the day I will change to a smaller, lighter Devon or perhaps even a lighter spoon.

Dave, a relative novice to this type of fishing, asks about our chances with the fly. He has done a little salmon fishing with a single-handed rod in Scotland but has never seen a fish taken on the double-handed rod. I explain that the river is far too high for consistent fly fishing but promise to give the fly a chance in the afternoon, even if the river does not fall appreciably.

Dave has brought with him an 8½ft (2.5m) hollow glass rod along with a Mitchell 300 spinning reel loaded with 8lb (3.5kg) line. The rod will suffice, but the reel is quite unsuitable. It will hold no more than about 80m of 15lb (6.5kg) line and the 8lb (3.5kg) line is far too light for the type of fishing which we will be doing. My concern is not entirely due to the size and power of our quarry, for I have seen 12lb (5.5kg) salmon landed on 8lb (3.5kg) line. Rather, it is due to the stresses and strains which the line will encounter, near the bottom, throughout a day's fishing in a swollen river in March. Hooking the river bed, snagging in weeds or submerged branches, rough rocks, stones and boulders, all add to the stresses on nylon and decrease its effective

strength. At the end of the day you may find that your new 8lb (3.5kg) nylon has, at certain frayed points, had its strength reduced by 10 or even 20 per cent. Therefore, play it safe and leave a good safety margin. There is every excuse for losing a large spring salmon but no excuse for leaving a 3in (7.5cm) piece of plastic attached to 1m of nylon, and a great ignorant lump of lead trailing out of the poor creature.

Luckily I have a spare fixed-spool reel containing 100m of 12lb (5.5kg) nylon and a further 100m of 10lb (4.5kg) backing. Hopefully, Dave will not be brought to the backing today.

We are now almost ready to make our assault on the river. Wrapped in good warm jumpers, Barbour jackets and thigh waders, we are well insulated against the cold. I have my tailer and I give Dave my long-handled net, with strict instructions that he is not to attempt to use it on his own, except in an emergency, and that if possible he should beach his fish rather than try to net it single-handed.

As we eagerly make our way across the wide ploughed field, we see our host for the day tackling up beside his car on the opposite bank. Despite protests from Dave, who is eager to get cracking, I insist that a few minutes spent discussing the water to be fished and results to date could well mean the difference between success and failure.

Fifteen minutes later we make our way upstream, brimming with confidence and well briefed on the pattern of fishing to date and the lies to concentrate on. Our stretch of water is primarily a long deep glide with some fast broken water at the head and one large deep pool (tastefully named the Bullock Hole) at the near end. Overall it is less than a kilometre in length. Our host advises us to ignore the faster water and to concentrate on the middle and lower portions of the beat. The fish are moving upstream close under the banks and the baits should be fished slow and deep as water temperatures are only 2 to 4°C.

We walk to the series of lies described by our host and begin to fish. Dave selects a 2½in (6cm) brown and gold wooden Devon and I insist that he fish the water first. I accompany him down the stretch, offering advice and carrying the all-important net.

At first, Dave is inclined to retrieve far too fast; he quickly reels in the bait when it is approximately three-quarters of the way across the 30m-wide river. However, he soon learns that the main principle of salmon fishing in moving water is to let the current do the work for you. You cast out and downstream at an angle of approximately 75°C and let the current take the bait and swing it into midstream. If you feel the bait touching the bottom, retrieve slowly until you feel the resistance on the lure increase, then let the current continue to do its work. Let the bait swing right into your bank, and if fishing a well-known salmon lie be sure to fish it from a position 30 or 40m upstream. This gives you plenty of room to manoeuvre the bait across the stream and into the lie. Use your imagination to visualise the salmon lying some 1 to 2m below the surface, pectoral fins just touching the bottom. Allow the lure to dangle tantalisingly in front of the lie and, if you wish, you can change the rhythm and movement of the lure by drawing the rod top towards you and then releasing it downstream. When fishing under your own bank the advantages of a long rod cannot be overemphasised. In the deeper pools it is, of course, necessary to constantly retrieve the spinner, but at a very slow pace.

Fishing carefully, it takes us almost two hours to reach the neck of the Bullock Hole and by this stage Dave is becoming disheartened. We have not encountered a single fish. Being a coarse angler at heart, Dave is used to somewhat faster action. I console him with tales of blank days saved by a single last cast and leave him to fish out the beat alone.

As I slowly fish down the beat, covering the stretch previously fished by Dave, I notice that the water looks even more cloudy than in the early morning. This I put down to melting snow in the Wicklow mountains, for we are approaching midday and blasts of watery sun are appearing from time to time. Slowly melting snow can bring a slight rise in water levels and encourage fresh fish to run, provided the melt is not accompanied by a great sudden flush of cold water. Normally, the high snows have begun to freeze over by mid-afternoon and the water begins to clear.

As I ponder my afternoon tactics my line suddenly stops and I feel a slow, even resistance down the line. I pause and lift into my first springer of the season. I call to Dave who is by this time making his way upstream towards me and he excitedly covers the remaining 100m in what seems like seconds.

The fish initially runs across and upstream into the current, a tactic salmon often employ when confused. Without warning, it turns tail and heads downstream in a long, deep, powerful run. Within seconds it has taken almost 80m of line from my reel and is well below us. Suddenly the fish stops and begins to splash on the surface and move aimlessly from bank to bank. I realise that I have hooked a kelt and not a fresh spring salmon, as I had first imagined. After about three or four minutes the poor fish is completely played out and heaved over on its great side. It is a well-mended kelt of perhaps nine or ten pounds, but in good condition; when it first entered the river the previous spring I am sure it would have weighed 15lb (6.5kg) or more.

Dave eagerly waits, with the net ready to do the needful. Since it is a kelt I decide to let Dave net him without any advice from me. He places the net in the water at an angle of 45°C and waits for me to bring the fish to him. Unused to landing fish of this size, he underestimates the time it takes to draw the fish across the net, and about two seconds too early he scoops with the net, lifting the great fish's tail clean out of the water; the fish slips off the rim

Neatly folded lazy beds slope gently towards a deep salmon holding pool on the River Erriff, Co. Mayo

Even the stately salmon may fall to the humble float-fished worm. Ballynahinch River, Co. Galway

It pays to know your lake. A fine fresh July grilse for two of Lough Currane's (Co. Kerry) most experienced gillies. Terence Wharton (with fish) and Brud Sullivan

of the net, hitting the line a resounding tap. The sudden wrench of the line loosens the hook-hold and the fish is free. Dave has made three basic mistakes in netting the salmon: firstly, he did not take care to conceal his presence on the bank by kneeling or crouching down; secondly, he neglected to sink the net well down in the water and to keep it parallel with the river bed; and thirdly, he scooped at the fish instead of waiting until it was drawn over the waiting net.

By this stage there is an obvious rise in the water level and I suggest to Dave that he should walk to the top of the beat and fish the fast water above the top run, a favourite place for salmon to lie. When I finally join him just before lunch I find a very despondent Dave sitting on the bank and looking as if suicide is not far from his mind. At his very first cast at the neck of the run he had hooked an 'enormous' salmon, but it had decided that salt water was preferable to fresh water and turned tail downstream, using the current and its own weight to strip line from his reel. Despite Dave's best efforts to dash downstream after the fish, it had taken out all of his main line and 20 or 30m of backing before it found a large weed-bed, dived underneath and struggled free, leaving the spinner behind. However, Dave is glad that he took my advice and resisted his own temptation to refill his small Mitchell with 80m of 15lb (6.5kg) line.

After lunch we again fish our beat separately, but by 3.00 pm we have had no further takes. As promised, I change to the fly and, using a 15ft (4.5m) Walker fly rod, a size 12 fast-sinking Air Cell line and a 10ft (3m) cast of 15lb (6.5kg) nylon, I fish the faster streamy water and the glides. I choose a 3in (7.5cm) aluminium tube fly, the Garry Dog, for no particular reason except that I think the size is right and I prefer some orange and yellow in my fly when the water is heavily coloured. When estimating the length of tube flies, remember to include the rubber or plastic shield which holds the treble in your

calculations, ie, a 3in (7.5cm) tube is really a 2½in (6cm) fly with an extra ½in (1cm) piece of rubber attached.

On the River Slaney there is a most peculiar rule which forbids wading before 1 May each season and so I am restricted to fishing from my own bank. It is no great problem today, but when the river is low and there is a strong wind blowing it would be a great advantage to fish down, using body waders and a good reliable wading staff.

I fish the more likely fly water several times, changing to both larger tube flies and flies tied on smaller Esmonde Drury trebles (Curry Shrimp, Hairy Mary, and Fox and Orange), but not surprisingly I get little response.

With the river starting to clear I decide to change back to the spinner and to try a 2½in (6cm) yellow belly Devon. On my first few casts I hook a salmon which plays hard in the strong current and takes a full ten minutes to land. Nothing spectacular in the fight, no jumps, no acrobatics, just a series of long deep runs. However, the fish is obviously fresh and very powerful. I finally subdue the salmon opposite a clean shelving bank of shingle and decide to show Dave the best method to use when beaching a salmon. With the fish well played out on his side, I move carefully to the water's edge, keeping the rod at arm's length. I enter the water a little above the fish and smartly move out until I am behind it. I then move towards the shore with the rod still at arm's length and pointing towards the gravel. The fish is thus drawn by the line inshore until his head is out of the water on the sand. I again move up behind the fish and catch him by the wrist of the tail, which affords an excellent holding point. I push the fish a little further up the gravel bank and lift my prize clean out of the water. A beautiful 10lb, fresh run silver salmon with sea lice clustered around its tail!

Despite fishing well into dusk we have no further success and must be contented with our single prize.

Grilse fishing

For me the best of the salmon fishing season starts in early June with the first influx of grilse, the one-sea-winter salmon which left the river only twelve months previously. These lively, agile fish enter the rivers from late May to September but most grilse fisheries have very definite seasons. In both the Shannon at Castleconnel, County Limerick, and in the Corrib, the main grilse run is over by late June. In spate rivers, such as the Erriff and the Bush, the grilse run continues throughout July, slows down somewhat in August but sees an additional spurt in early September, particularly during drought years when fish may be largely confined to the estuary between mid-July and early September. In the River Feale in County Kerry, in contrast, the main grilse run only starts in early to mid-August and, as mentioned previously, there has been a tendency in recent years for an autumn run of grilse to appear in many of the southern rivers (Suir, Barrow, Nore, Blackwater, etc) during mid to late August.

The River Corrib is a much favoured haunt of both anglers and fish-watchers. This short river forms the gateway to L. Corrib's 44,000 acres and on occasion large numbers of salmon and grilse may be seen lingering in the pools below the weir

Electrical fishing is one of the most important management techniques. Here the author samples a small sea trout spawning stream in Co. Donegal

One of the magnificent specimen sea trout for which Lough Currane is justly famous — a seven-pounder taken on a size 10 Claret Bumble

Delicately camouflaged against the gravel-laden stream bed, these young trout are almost invisible to predators

A handsome selection of salmon and sea trout flies (tyings by Peter O'Reilly)

Soaked to the skin but content. A nice plump grilse is a just reward for this tenacious angler on the Glenamoy River, Co. Mayo

33

If you hit the grilse when they are in taking mood, they are almost as easy to catch as mackerel. I remember some years ago on the River Erriff catching three grilse and losing three others in just over one hour. During the same period my brother landed two fish and lost two others. However, grilse go stale very fast and can become very dour overnight, quite in contrast to the spring fish. This may be largely due to higher water temperatures in summer, but there is still no real evidence as to why it occurs.

Grilse range in size from 2½ to 9lb (1–4kg), with some autumn fish up to 10lb (4.5kg), but the average size is generally around 5lb (2.5kg). They are exceptionally lively and will often jump and run with amazing agility. They are at their very best on a single-handed fly rod.

Timing is important

Research has shown that, in general, grilse move at night, and the best time to catch a fish, in moderate to low water, is for an hour around dawn or dusk. Unlike sea trout, they take poorly at night and although the odd fish is taken whilst sea trout fishing, it is generally not considered worthwhile to fish for grilse after dark.

The best time to encounter grilse is during a dropping summer flood. They tend not to take during a rising flood, except for a very short period as the river begins to rise. However, during the latter two-thirds of the spate there is a general movement upstream and even red, stale fish may take at this time. My father has long maintained that in short spate rivers and in the lower sections of the larger spring rivers, salmon are greatly influenced by the lunar cycle and that fish often take around the time of high tide, regardless of the height of the water and the distance from the sea. Recent research has shown a strong correlation in the number of salmon caught per day and the number of high tide periods falling within the average day fished. The numbers taken are also closely clustered around high tide — even eight miles from the sea! My dad's response to all of this is a simple 'I told you so'. For my own part I tend to fish that little bit harder around high tide in recent years, but please yourself!

EQUIPMENT

Fly rods

The grilse angler should ideally be equipped with two rods: a 12–14ft (3.5–4m) double-handed rod for use in high water or strong winds and a 9½–11ft (3–3.5m) single-handed rod for use under all other conditions. However, if I were limited to one rod, I would choose the single-handed type. Lightness and strength are obvious requirements in such rods and carbon fibre is by far the most suitable material to choose. The rods should be strong and capable of handling both summer salmon up to 12 or 15lb (5.5–6.5kg) and the small 3–8lb (1.5–3.5kg) grilse.

Spinning rods

When spinning for grilse, a full action, single or double-handed, 8–10ft (2.5–3m) carbon fibre or fibreglass rod is used. I prefer a rather stiff rod which is capable of landing a fish in a reasonable length of time, even when the river is flowing hard and fast. A slightly longer rod has considerable advantages if you also intend to fish either the worm or the prawn.

Fly reels

These vary in diameter from 3½ to 4in (9–10cm) but the most important feature is that the reel of your choice should have the capacity to hold a size 8–10 double-tapered fly line and some 100m of 15–20lb (6.5–9kg) braided nylon backing. A good strong ratchet and conveniently located drag control are also essential. In my experience a grilse rarely takes you to the backing, but when the occasion does arise you should be confident that the knot joining the backing and the main line will slip easily to and fro through the rod rings. It is particularly important to check this in the case of a single-handed rod, where the top rings are frequently of a narrow diameter.

Spinning reels

Any good quality, medium sized, fixed-spool reel will suffice when spinning for grilse. As in the case of spring fishing, the drag control should be sensitive and readily accessible. The reel should be loaded with 150–200m of 8–12lb (3.5–5.5kg) nylon. Since most spinning for grilse is carried out under high water conditions in summer, I would prefer to use heavier nylon of 10–12lb (4.5–5.5kg) breaking strain. Fishing a fast-moving Mepps upstream, under low water conditions, can be very exciting and in such situations I would fish the lighter 8lb (3.5kg) monofilament.

Fly lines

A similar range of lines to that described for spring salmon fishing is available for grilse fishing. However, a floating line and a sink-tip line of the appropriate density will deal with all but the most extreme situations. The sink-tip is used under conditions of high water or strong wind, while the floating line is used under calm or low water conditions. In the cooler waters of late autumn (mid to late September), a slow sinking line can prove very useful in locating those dour, stale fish which hug the bottom of the pools.

Leaders (casts)

In spate rivers, which also contain sea trout, a dropper is frequently added to the leader or cast. A salmon fly is fished on the point and a sea trout fly on the bob. Using a dropper can result in a grilse snagging the loose fly during the fight, but the angler must choose whether or not he is willing to accept this risk. I normally fish a tapered cast for grilse, consisting of approximately equal proportions of 15, 12 and 10lb (7, 5.5 and 4.5kg) monofilament. I use a 10–12ft (3–4m) cast on my double-handed 14ft (4m) rod and an 8–9ft (2.5–3m) cast on the 9½ft (3m) single-handed rod.

Dapping the daddy-long-legs on Doo Lough, Co. Mayo

A heart-stopping moment — the rise of a good limestone trout. River Shiven, Co. Galway (Photo by the author)

A mayfly dun nestles into a safe refuge

On a stream there is no substitute for delicate presentation. Jimmy Whelan casts a true line on the Little Brosna River, Co. Tipperary

A minnow bottle proves its worth

TECHNIQUES OF GRILSE FISHING

It is mid-July and I am lucky enough to be fishing for two days on the River Erriff in County Mayo. When the state took over the fishery in 1982 it was heavily poached both in fresh water and in the long, fiord-like Killary Harbour, into which both the Erriff and the neighbouring Bundorragh (Delphi System) rivers flow. In just five years the fishery has been transformed, with total rod catches reaching 870 salmon by 1988 and the CPUE varying between .25 and .50 over the same period. Not bad for a mere eight miles of smallish spate river!

On arrival I find that a large flood occurred the previous weekend and that there are plenty of fish in the river. The counter has consistently recorded twenty to forty grilse each night and so a steady dribble of really sea-fresh fish are also coming through. The river is still higher than normal for July but the water is running very clear.

It is now 6.00 am and I am just about to tackle up at the car before making my way down through the rough, rambling fields to the river bank. I know the beat to which I have been allocated quite well and I am in no doubt about the tactics I will employ. I quickly assemble my tackle which consists of a strong 9½ft (3m) single-handed rod and a forward-tapered floating line attached to 100m of 30lb (13.5kg) braided nylon backing. I am also carrying a spare reel-spool containing a sink-tip, forward-tapered line attached to a similar length and strength of backing.

The water is running clear, so I choose a size 8, double Blue Charm for the tail and a size 10 Black Pennell (on a trout hook) for the dropper. There is hardly a puff of wind, so I propose to concentrate on the running water before breakfast and to move to the flats later in the morning if the wind rises sufficiently.

I approach the water's edge carefully, for I learned a very valuable lesson some years ago when walking

one of the lower Erriff beats. I came upon one of the Erriff 'regulars' who was just about to start fishing a section of the beat known as the General's Reach. As I approached from the pool below, he asked me to keep well back from the edge of the bank. I waited to watch him fishing the 'Generals', as I was keen to find out exactly how, over the years, he had consistently managed to figure amongst the best rods. To my amazement he stalked the edge of the pool as if he was trout fishing, and shooting a short line upstream he carefully covered every gap in a long bed of pondweed (*Potamogeton*) which lies underneath the left bank at this point. At times, he was a metre or more back from the edge of the bank and for all intents and purposes fishing by touch. In a matter of twenty minutes he hooked a 6lb (2.5kg) grilse, which I dutifully landed, and a second smaller fish which was so close to the bank that it landed momentarily on the lower, secondary peat bank following its initial jump; this fish he eventually lost but he rose two others. Quite some performance from a stretch which is normally fished from the left bank by casting a long line to the 'well-known lies' on the right bank!

Fishing the near water first, I gradually move my flies out towards the far bank. When I am satisfied that no taking fish are in my immediate vicinity, I begin to fish my flies across and down. Traditionally, one is supposed to cast one's flies across the run at an angle of about 75° and to mend the line so that the current takes the flies in an even arc from near the far bank to a point some 10 to 20m below where you are fishing, depending on the length of your cast. However, I have found that in all but the fastest water a broken retrieve, alternating between the classic 'mended line approach' and a figure-of-eight, trout-type retrieve (particularly in pool areas) has served me best. I would agree with Falkus when he states that the fly should be fishing some 4 to 6in (10–15cm) below the surface as it goes over the fish's lie.

I fish the two main areas of broken water on the beat between 6.00 and 9.00 am, and apart from a nice plump sea trout of approximately 10oz (280g) and a few splashes in the flats below me, I see little activity.

Having breakfasted back in the lodge I return to the beat to find that the gentleman with whom I am to share the beat for the day has arrived. He is fishing the fast water which I fished previously. Having exchanged a few pleasantries I make my way towards the flats, where a good westerly breeze has developed. The sky is still quite overcast but it is forecast to brighten and clear later in the morning and so I feel that my best chance of a salmon is within the next hour or so.

A westerly wind is directly upstream and the only really pleasant way to fish is either squarely across or more frequently, slightly upstream, with the prevailing wind. In the flats, particularly when the water level is normal or a little above, I am convinced that a good breeze sets up secondary currents, for at times the behaviour of both the line and the fish would deceive you into thinking that you were in fact fishing downstream.

After about fifteen minutes I notice a very fine head and tail rise about half way across the river and slightly above where I am standing. I quickly move up into position and fish carefully over the spot where I saw the fish move. After three casts there is still no response. Just as I am about to take my flies out of the water, I notice a movement under my own bank, behind my flies. I cast short, covering the spot where I noticed the movement. Suddenly there is a strong pull and I am into my first Erriff salmon of the season. The fish splashes hard on the surface several times before making a determined dash across to the far bank. This gives me time to retrieve some loose line which is lying on the ground in front of me and enables me to take the fish on the reel. After a lively, fast fight lasting two or three minutes, the fish tires and begins slowly to topple over on its side. I have the net ready and as the fish passes over the rim I lift decisively. The salmon is about 3lb (1.5kg) in weight and reasonably fresh run. Certainly not a monster, but a welcome catch none the less. Some minutes later I hook a second, much larger fish well out in the river, but the hook-hold pulls free before I get a chance to assess the fish's weight.

Soon after this, a strong sun makes its appearance from behind the clouds, and although I fish on well into the afternoon, no more salmon come my way. Around teatime heavy black clouds begin to gather and by 6.00 pm it is really bucketing rain. The wind has also begun to rise and is now gusting force 7 or 8. I am tired after my long day and I retire to the lodge for a rest and some welcome hot food.

Later that evening I discuss the events of the day with my companion who has shared the beat with me. He had caught nothing by 6.00 pm when the storm broke and so he decided that he would fish the worm for a while before returning to the lodge. After about half an hour he noticed that the river was starting to rise quickly and to discolour. So he changed from leger tactics to a light float and moved down to the top of the flats. Almost immediately he lost a small fish due to striking too soon. Some minutes later he hooked and landed a fine 10½lb (5kg) cock fish which had probably resided in the flat since March or April. Although he fished for a further half an hour, he encountered no more salmon. He had been fortunate enough to be on the spot for that most fickle of times, the first few inches of the fresh flood.

The next morning the river is a metre above normal and highly coloured. It rained throughout the night, clearing only at about 6.00 am.

My beat for the day is approximately one and a half kilometres long and contains a good mixture of deep flats, pools and fast ripply water. When I arrive at the beat I find that the water is pushing through the eye of the bridge with tremendous force

*Imitative trout fly
patterns. Subtle and
sombre, their purpose is
to deceive, not merely
attract (tyings by
Brendan Whelan)*

*One of the most
beautiful salmon and sea
trout loughs in Ireland.
Derryclare Lough,
Connemara, Co.
Galway*

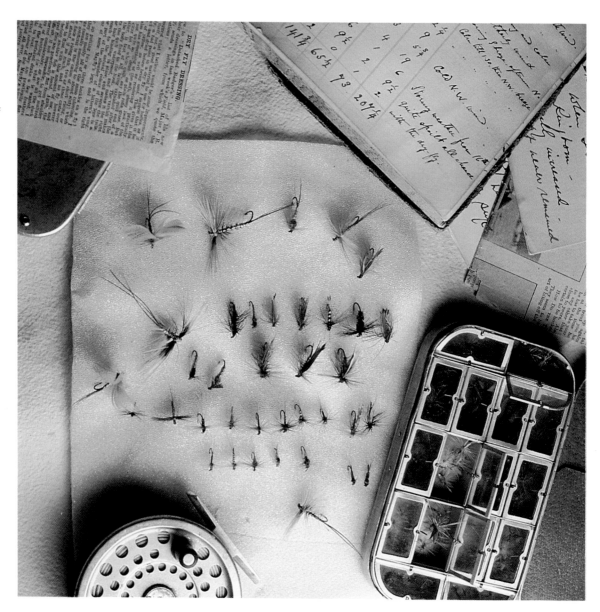

and on down through the rocky gulley at the neck of the pool. Where the large bridge-pool levels out I notice a series of attractive eddies which I know cover banks of clean gravel. Under normal conditions the water here is just a few centimetres deep, but in today's flood it seems a likely area for travelling salmon to rest.

Because of the heavy brown colour in the water and the exceptionally strong northwest wind, which would make effective fly casting difficult, I decide to spin. To start with I intend to use a ¼oz (7g) silver Toby on a light 9ft (2.5m) spinning rod and 10lb (4.5kg) main line. I have found this bait to be very effective in brown flood water; an added advantage of the smaller bait is that it also attracts sea trout. To ensure that the bait fishes well down in the flooded water, I thread on a ½oz (14g) bullet lead between the upper swivel and the anti-kink. As the river drops I can dispense entirely with the lead.

I make my way down the bank, ignoring the rushing, tumbling water in the neck of the bridge-pool and station myself about 30m above the swirling eddies. Unlike spring fish, grilse seem to delight in a dancing, wavering bait some 4 to 12in (10–30cm) below the surface and will often rise at a lure. For this reason I always fish the silver Toby with either a quick sink-and-draw or a fast flashing motion. The fish normally hit the bait very hard and so your slipping clutch needs to be carefully set.

As I move the bait through the water towards the eddy I feel a sharp pluck. I lift the rod tip but sense no resistance. Almost immediately the rod tip jerks decisively and I am into a strong ¾lb (340g) sea trout. The fish is quickly landed and dispatched.

I cast out for a second cast, delighted with my initial success, and move the spinner across the pool towards the swirling series of eddies. I spin across the most likely area, anticipating the sudden lunge of a fresh fish, but nothing happens. I fish down through the eddies, disappointed at the lack of a fish. Near the tail of the pool, somewhat separated from the others, I find a single eddy swirling in a more determined fashion, its surface flecked with white froth. Having fished through the foam-covered area, I am just about to lift the spinner from the water when there is a ferocious splash and I am into a salmon. The fish dashes across into the main current at the tail of the pool and splashes on the surface. It then falters for a second, as if considering its next move, and makes an equally determined run towards its lie under my own bank. I move back from the water's edge so as not to disturb the fish and the remainder of the battle takes place within 10 or 15m of the bank. After two or three minutes the grilse has all but exhausted itself in the fast current and is quickly drawn over the waiting net. My spring balance records 4½lb (2kg).

For the next two hours I fish from pool to pool with the silver Toby, but apart from another small sea trout I see no further evidence of any salmon.

By early afternoon the day has brightened somewhat, the wind has abated slightly and the water is appreciably clearer. I change to the fly and fishing my single-handed rod, a size 8 sink-tip line, a Curry Shrimp (double) on the tail and a size 10 Dunkeld on the dropper, I slowly fish my way downstream. The wind makes casting exceptionally difficult, but by facing across and slightly downstream I manage to cover approximately half the river's width. The strong current works the flies beautifully and I am quite content that the important lies under my own bank are being well covered. Some 500m down from the bridge-pool is a small holding pool situated under a high clay bank. It is a productive area, particularly under high water conditions, and the outer lies are normally fished from a series of gravel banks situated along the left bank. I wade out onto the firm gravel at the neck of the pool and fish around in an arc, slowly making my way towards the tail of the pool. As the flies swing away from the high bank, towards the centre of the pool, the line tightens. I instinctively lift the rod but I am careful not to strike. The line goes slack and completes its arc towards the left bank. I carefully examine both the dropper and the tail fly but I can see no reason for the fish's refusal. I cast again and before I have a chance to even mend the line there is a solid take. The tail of the fish appears momentarily above the surface as the salmon turns and races downstream. Within seconds the fish has reached the tail of the short pool and after just a split second of hesitation it blunders down into the shallow rocky water above the lower pool. The fish dashes into the body of the pool, as I clamber towards the bank and quickly move downstream, madly retrieving lost line. By the time I reach the pool's edge the fish has settled on the bottom and I can only sense a slow rhythmic throb at the end of the line. Despite increased pressure the fish steadfastly refuses to move. I then adopt a useful trick learned many years ago when retrieving trout from weedbeds in the Kells Blackwater. I point the rod at the fish and tap sharply on the cork handle. This irritates the hook-hold and the fish shoots forward and arches out of the water in a most spectacular jump. A strong determined fight follows, but some five minutes later the fish is ready to be landed. Because of the shallowness of the water and the firm shelving gravel beds along my own bank, I decide to beach the fish. It is a fine fresh grilse weighing some 6½lb (3kg) and to my surprise I find that it has taken the size 10 Dunkeld intended for sea trout. There really is no accounting for taste!

Stillwater salmon fishing

Fly fishing for grilse in still water, during the summer months, is generally combined with sea trout fishing and the angler will find all of the necessary detail in Chapter 3. However, it is worth making the point at this stage that salmon often reside in very specific lies in a lake. They are often found over sand or gravel banks, particularly if they are adjacent to an inflowing stream. Salmon also lie at the points of natural rock or stone jetties protruding out into the lake. Favourite lies are normally close inshore where the water is only one or two metres deep. For some reason salmon seem to love large boulders and invariably each sea trout lough in the west of Ireland seems to have at least one 'salmon rock'.

Grilse are normally taken on standard sea trout flies. However, if one suspects a fresh run of salmon or conditions are ideal (strong wind accompanied by a large, slow swell), then either a bushy size 8 Green Peter or a Daddy-long-legs should adorn the top dropper.

Ireland possesses several excellent spring salmon loughs (Currane, Beltra, Killarney, etc) and these may provide sport from mid-January to late April or early May. It is traditional to troll for salmon during the early part of the season and to commence fly fishing in March (for details of trolling methods, see pages 128 and 221).

1. *The retrieve*
2. *The rise*

3. *The take*
4. *The strike*

Sunset on a sheltered corner of Lough Corrib, Co. Galway

45

EQUIPMENT

Fly fishing for spring salmon on still waters is a strange business and one can see an array of tackle in use, from the traditional double-handed rod to standard 10–11ft (3-3.5m) trout fly rods. One should not be too quick to decry the use of traditional tackle as unnecessarily cumbersome, for spring salmon are found in very specific lies and the ability to cast a long accurate line can often be of great advantage. There is one particular salmon lie near the mouth of the inflowing Cummeragh River on Lough Currane, where the salmon take up station in the gap between a large and a small boulder. To fish this lie, the boat must be held off by one angler (or the gillie) while the lie is fished by a double-handed rod.

Like the grilse, salmon are often found in quite shallow water and so the use of fast-sinking lines is generally unnecessary. However, a slow-sinking or sink-tip line is often used. Large lakes in spring are invariably inhospitable places covered by large rolling waves and since these spring fish are not much inclined to dash about after lures or flies, the fly should be drawn squarely across their lie.

Anglers new to spring salmon fishing in lakes should be warned that there are no river banks to confine the movements of these large fish and runs of 100m or more are not uncommon; agility with the oars or engine and 100m or more of backing are often called for.

To my mind the ideal tackle consists of a strong (reservoir-type) 9½–10ft (3m) trout or grilse fly rod, a large reel (eg 4½in Super Condex), a size 8 or 9 sink-tip line and at least 100m of braided nylon backing. The leader should consist of 15–18lb (6.5–8kg) nylon. When stillwater fishing for salmon a dropper is often used, and indeed on some west of Ireland fisheries it is considered almost compulsory. Spring salmon flies are legion but I would advise sizes 2 to 6, either singles or doubles. Tube flies are little used in still waters but are deserving of more widespread use; some anglers have in recent years enjoyed considerable success using tubes from a boat.

Finally, I would advise anyone contemplating a day's salmon fishing on still water to bring along a good competent gillie. These large lakes are no place for the inexperienced, and both in terms of safety and local knowledge, a good boatman is an invaluable addition to the party.

Beat 4 on the River Erriff, Co. Mayo. A favourite lie for both fresh grilse and large sea trout

Alternative grilse fishing methods

There are times when the salmon angler finds that his quarry is unresponsive to either fly or spinner and it is then that he must consider turning his attentions to the use of the worm, prawn or shrimp. The ethics of bait-fishing for salmon have, over the years, been hotly debated and there is a school of thought which claims that it is not quite 'the thing' to catch your salmon on anything other than the artificial fly. While this may be quite a legitimate stance for those fortunate enough to have access to regular salmon fishing and who can make the most of ideal water conditions, they should consider the visiting angler who has few such opportunities and must make the most of his twice- or thrice-yearly visits. It is my own view that it is far more reasonable to limit the number of salmon taken on a particular method than to ban the method altogether; for it is not the method *per se* but rather the angler using it which causes the abuse.

On the Erriff and Ballynahinch fisheries in the west of Ireland there is an admirable rule whereby a guest who has not succeeded in catching a salmon on the fly by 5.00 pm may, if he chooses, bait fish until 7.00 pm. He is, however, strictly limited to one fish on the Erriff and two on Ballynahinch and must revert to fly fishing once he has taken his quota.

Worm fishing

I have many fond memories of worm fishing for salmon. My first ever salmon was taken on the worm in the River Rye, a tributary of the River Liffey, in Dublin. We arrived at the river around 5.00 pm and because of the calm June weather my brother and I had keen expectations of a strong evening rise of brown trout. After consuming some sandwiches and a flask of tea we decided to reconnoitre our chosen stretch. As we stood beside a deep pool watching for evidence of trout feeding, a large fish broke the water in the neck of the pool. For several minutes he continued to move around the pool in a most playful manner, flashing his silver flanks and, at times, splashing on the surface. A large trout fly was quickly stripped of fur and feather and a few minutes work amongst the grass tufts provided us with two large black-headed worms. Since my fly rod was the stronger of the two, I was selected as *the* angler.

By this time the fish had settled and we had no idea where he was lying. I went to the neck of the pool and cast in my worms. Almost instantly the fish swam across the pool in a great bow wave and grabbed the worms before they had even touched the bottom. I had the good sense to give him line and he moved back to his lie. There he played with the worms with a biting, nipping motion, for a full five minutes. Suddenly he lunged back across the pool and arched out of the water. I instinctively struck and the great fish was mine. We finished that evening with a total

Heavily spotted and displaying that most characteristic magenta flush, this fine rainbow was taken in Pallas Lake, Co. Offaly

Some less than subtle rainbow lures (tyings by the author)

of ten brown trout (up to 1¾lb; 800g), all taken on spent olive, and my 8½lb (4kg) salmon. Not a bad evening's work for two teenage boys.

The worm is principally a bait of extreme water conditions, when the river is either too high or too low for the fly or spinner. In high water conditions it is generally fished close into the bank and amongst well-known salmon lies. In these conditions the local angler has a definite advantage, for he knows from experience where to expect a resting salmon and can make the best use of his time. The visiting angler must fish all of the likely areas, remembering to keep his bait fishing close to the bank.

One often finds local anglers perched on the river bank, fishing a stationary worm into a well-known lie. Here they will sit for hours or even days, quite confident that a fish will eventually take the worm. I am afraid I find little to interest me in this form of fishing.

I prefer to fish the worm on a leger tackle or on a float tackle and to carefully fish all of the water available to me. I have found that in contrast to my initial experience with the worm, salmon rarely take it when it first moves past their noses and it is worth taking some time to fish each lie. You may use either your fly rod or your spinning rod when worm fishing but the latter is best under high water conditions when a half ounce (14g) or more of lead may be required.

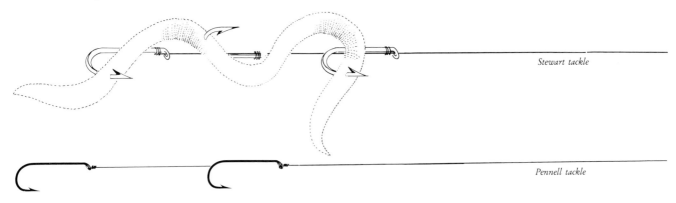

Stewart tackle

Pennell tackle

The two worms should be mounted on a single hook, leaving plenty of 'tails', and the bait should be kept as near as possible to the bottom. When a fish takes, you will sense an initial tremor followed by a soft tapping sensation — not the firm knock, knock, knock you get from a trout. The salmon will often leave his lie and follow the worm right into your bank. Always avoid retrieving your worm too soon. As the fish moves back towards his lie, feed him the appropriate length of line. When the fish has finally settled into his lie, strike firmly.

Under exceptionally low water conditions the worm should be fished on a long sensitive rod — a fly rod is ideal. The worms may be mounted as described previously or else a double-hook Pennell or Stewart tackle can be used. This provides the advantage that it merely lip-hooks smaller fish, such as salmon or trout parr, and these may be safely returned to the water. Weight is normally provided by a series of split-shot or a very small leger. This method is particularly successful in clear, fast water.

When float fishing the worm, a stop knot should be used and the float continuously re-set in line with the differing contours of the river bed. Again, the object of the exercise is to ensure that the worm rolls past the salmon in as natural a fashion as possible. Incidentally, one should not become too concerned if, after twenty minutes or so, the worms become moribund, for salmon do not necessarily react positively to large, active worms. In some instances the reverse may be true and they actually prefer a limp bait!

Prawns and shrimps

In my experience nothing causes so much dissent or acrimony amongst salmon anglers as the question of fishing the natural prawn or shrimp. Let me nail my colours to the mast straight away and put forward my own strongly held view that, in heavily fished association or syndicate waters, the use of these baits should be strictly controlled. I hark back here to my earlier statement that bag limits are the fairest and most efficient means of regulating bait fishing. If this strategy fails to curb the numbers of salmon taken by these methods, then there is every reason to ban the use of the techniques altogether.

One might imagine from the above that a prawn or shrimp is almost guaranteed to provide one with a fish. I have found this to be far from the truth. However, when fish are taking baits, an experienced angler can account for four or five salmon in a few hours' fishing. This is particularly true when fresh grilse are running, for at such times they are very susceptible to a shrimp fished on a float.

There is often confusion with regard to the differences between a prawn (*Leander serratus*) and a shrimp (*Leander squilla*). As far as the angler is concerned, the only real difference is size. The prawn can reach a length of 8in (20cm) or more while the shrimp rarely grows much bigger than 3in (7.5cm). The ideal size for a prawn is around 5in (13cm) and a shrimp around 2in (5cm); all the better if the creatures are in berry, that is to say, have a clump of succulent eggs between their legs. Ideally the baits should be fresh, but for those of us who must make do with preserved animals, frozen or salted baits are probably best. They are fished from April through to September but are rarely successful when water temperatures are much below 10°C.

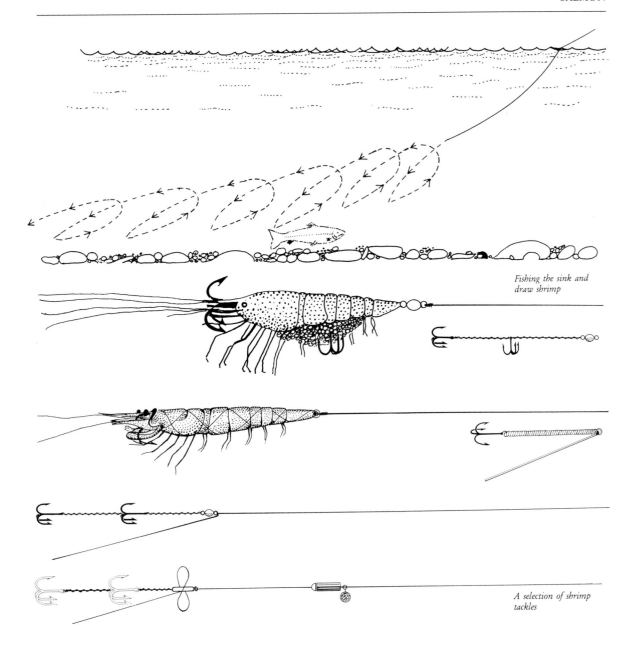

Fishing the sink and draw shrimp

A selection of shrimp tackles

One often hears horror stories regarding the effect which a prawn may have on a pool of salmon. There is no doubt that it can disturb or even frighten fish from their lies, but although such an event may disturb the fish for a short while, I am quite sure it does no long-term harm. In a situation where you are sharing the beat with other anglers, particularly if they are fly fishing, you should refrain from using the prawn without first obtaining the agreement of your neighbour.

The methods normally used when prawn or shrimp fishing include spinning, trotting, drift-lining and sink-and-draw. My own favourite is the sink-and-draw method. This is probably due, however, less to its inherent efficacy than to memories of my ill-spent youth when many pleasant hours were devoted to fishing the natural minnow in a similar fashion.

Drift-lining is an interesting method frequently used in the Munster Blackwater. The shrimp is mounted in a similar manner to that shown for the sink-and-draw method (whiskers facing away from the line). The bait is weighted according to the depth and power of the water being fished. The object is to keep the bait moving in a natural manner along or close to the bed of the river. The shrimp is cast across the river and slightly upstream. The bait is then slowly twitched along the bottom as the line is swept downstream in a broad arc by the current. When the line is directly below the angler the bait is retrieved in a slow sink-and-draw manner. If a fish should take, give him line until he reaches his lie; then a smart strike and the fish is yours.

During the summer months there is no substitute for the float-fished shrimp. When shrimp fishing, one often sees anglers using great red and white floats (fit for sharks), chunks of lead, sea swivels and 15 or 20lb (6.5–9kg) nylon. They invariably catch salmon, a sure proof that salmon are certainly not gut-shy! However, salmon are very sensitive to the resistance which such tackle may generate. For that reason, the experienced coarse angler using a properly mounted waggler and 8lb (3.5kg) nylon will encounter far more solid takes than his traditional counterpart. The rule of thumb when float-fishing the shrimp is to strike at the first dip of the float; for at this stage the salmon will have sucked in the bait and a swift strike will ensure that he is hooked in the roof of the mouth. Some anglers fish the shrimp on a large single, size 2 or 4, but my own preference is for a 10 or 12 treble. With regard to binding material, I find that clear elastic thread is by far the best.

The colour of the shrimp or prawn seems all important at times and one should be guided by local knowledge when considering the use of either the natural pink prawn or the dyed purple or red prawn. For example, anglers along the Munster Blackwater claim that a natural shrimp should be used during low water conditions but that salmon prefer a purple shrimp immediately following a flood.

Whatever fears one might have regarding disturbing salmon with a prawn, the angler need have no such worries when fishing a shrimp. In my experience the carefully fished shrimp causes as little disturbance to a pool as a large fly on a sinking line.

CHAPTER 3

SEA TROUT

Life cycle and biology

Origin and evolution

Sea trout, or white trout (*Breac geal*) as they are often called in rural Ireland, are to be found in most estuaries or bays around our coast. It was originally thought that sea trout were a separate species to the non-migratory, ubiquitous brown trout (*Salmo fario*) and so they were designated as *Salmo trutta*. In more recent times taxonomists have decided that sea trout are no more than the migratory form of the brown trout and both are known as *Salmo trutta*. However, behaviourally the sea trout are quite distinct from the brown trout and for that reason alone I would agree with Hugh Falkus's suggestion that they should be clearly differentiated and that the brown trout should be known as *Salmo trutta fario* and the sea trout as *Salmo trutta trutta*.

Recent genetic work indicates that all present-day natural brown trout (non-anadromous) and sea trout populations, in Ireland and Britain, arose from a common ancestor. This anadromous species of trout probably first entered fresh water after the end of the last Ice Age, some 10 000 years ago. The enigma of why some trout will migrate to feed in the sea while others remain resident in fresh water still remains unresolved.

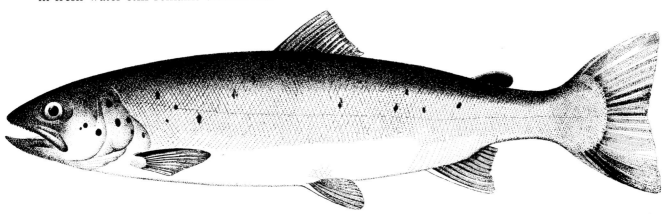

In all sea trout populations studied to date, females dominate. The ratio of females to males may vary from 60:40 per cent to 80:20 per cent, but in all cases it is the egg-laying female which is most likely to migrate to the sea. It is tempting to speculate on the survival value to the species of this adaptation but in reality we have little real basis for such conjecture. It is obvious, however, that the resident male brown trout play a far greater role in the maintenance of our sea trout stocks than was previously imagined. Indeed, the majority of female brown trout in these acid waters may be sea trout parr, which will ultimately migrate to the sea. The conservation of all juvenile brown trout within sea trout fisheries is therefore of major importance. Such a policy is in direct contrast with that recommended by Nall (1931) who considered such small or very small brown trout a nuisance. He wrote:

The remedy in Connemara would seem to be to net out and destroy the super abundance of small brown trout, which are mischievous, not only because they consume large proportions of the available food, but also because they devour the ova of the salmon and sea trout at spawning time.

Doo Lough, Co. Mayo. Part of the Delphi fishery, made famous by the writings of the late T C Kingsmill-Moore. Doo Lough is renowned for the abundance and quality of its sea trout

Location

Sea trout are plentiful in most short rivers running directly into the sea and in coastal lakes. They are seldom found far upstream in large rivers, although they may be numerous in the estuary, and they are essentially fish of acid waters (pH 5.5–6.5). In general, sea trout populations flourish where growth rates are poor and where survival in fresh water is difficult or where there is easy access to the sea. Although normally associated with salmon, there are many major salmon fisheries where sea trout are confined to the estuaries or the estuarine tributaries (eg the Rivers Slaney, Blackwater, Moy, etc). On the other hand, there are many lesser streams or small lake systems that do not hold many salmon, but in which sea trout are numerous.

Anadromous life cycle

Sea trout normally spend one to five years feeding in fresh water before migrating to the sea for the first time. In some fisheries (eg Lough Currane) sea trout smolts as large as 12in (30cm) have been recorded, but in general they are 6 to 10in (15–25cm). Out of every hundred smolts examined, 56 per cent would be two-year-old smolts, 37 per cent three-year-olds, 6 per cent four-year-olds and 1 per cent five-year-olds. Year-old sea trout smolts do exist but are rare. The main migration is in spring but a supplementary autumn seaward movement of small brown trout (non-smolts) has also been recorded from several Irish fisheries.

When sea trout leave their native rivers they normally feed, in shoals, close inshore along beaches, headlands and in estuaries. Their diet consists of small crustaceans, sandeels, herring fry, sprat and small pollack.

Once they have entered fresh water, sea trout feed intermittently, if at all, and lose condition exceptionally fast. A fish which enters fresh water weighing 3lb (1.5kg) may lose 8 to 12oz (230–340g) within four to eight weeks. Comparative samples of fish caught by draft net along the west coast show condition factors similar to those recorded along the east coast. Rod-caught sea trout, however, display a significantly poorer condition factor.

Many sea trout return to fresh water after feeding for three to five months in the sea. These sea trout are known by various local names: harvesters, juners, clowns, whitling or more commonly finnock. (The term 'finnock' is thought to have derived from the Gaelic term *fionn óg* meaning the fair or white young one.) More correctly they are called post-smolts and are the dominant age group in many Irish rivers. They normally average 8–10oz (230–280g) in weight. In many fisheries only a small proportion (10 to 20 per cent) of these post-smolts spawn, although significant numbers do over-winter in fresh water. It is not known what contribution these sea trout make in subsequent years to the commercial or rod catch, or indeed to the spawning stock.

Other sea trout return as maidens after spending one full year feeding in the sea. These fish normally average 1–1½lb (450–680g). Both one- and two-sea-winter maiden sea trout constitute the principal spawning stock in many Irish fisheries.

Spawning

Sea trout generally spawn in early to mid-November, some three to four weeks before the salmon. The pattern of redd construction, egg laying and mating is similar to that of the salmon. Sea trout often spawn in tiny streams and it is not unusual to find a 3 to 4lb (1.5–2kg) sea trout spawning in an insignificant brook, less than a metre wide and only 10 to 12in (25–30cm) deep (when in full spate!). The fish often enter such streams on a rising flood and within four to six hours have completed spawning and returned to their parent lake or river. The majority of sea trout fry spend only the first summer feeding in these tiny tributaries before migrating to the parent system. Nature has designed the sea trout to make full use of water courses which no self-respecting salmon would even consider as a potential home for their young.

Unlike salmon, sea trout normally survive the rigours of spawning, and fish which have spawned five times or more are not an uncommon feature of Irish fisheries. Sea trout kelts may return to the sea immediately after spawning but in general the majority of fish migrate in late March or April. In some years low water temperatures or drought conditions may delay this migration until May. These multi-spawners may spend only ten to twelve weeks feeding in the sea before returning to fresh water in mid to late July. They are little more than egg-laying machines, rather like the queen bee which stores up food and energy reserves for no other purpose than the procreation of the species. Little wonder, then, that these large multi-spawners feed little, if at all, in fresh water and are exceptionally dour and difficult to catch on rod and line.

After their first spawning, sea trout are normally annual spawners. The larger sizes of sea trout are therefore a mixture of maiden fish, which have been at sea for a year or more, and previously spawned fish, which are returning to fresh water for the second or third time.

Stocks and management

Drift and draft net fisheries

Unlike salmon, the majority of fish are taken in the angling fishery and at times up to 70 per cent of the total declared catch may be taken in this manner. The majority of these fish are the smaller finnock.

Traditionally, the draft net fishery took approximately 33 per cent of the declared catch and 4 to 7 per cent was shared between the drift nets and other commercial engines. It has been argued that the majority of larger sea trout enter the fisheries in the period mid-April to June and that the drift net fishery has little effect on the overall stock of these larger fish. However, apart from the Currane fishery in County Kerry, where the larger, previously spawned sea trout run in May and June, data from other west coast fisheries has shown that the larger fish may enter fresh water at any time from late June to early October, but principally in mid to late July when the salmon drift nets are most active.

Both the drift and draft net fisheries are size selective. Sea trout smaller than 3lb (1.5kg) are missing from the drift net catch, while those smaller than 1½lb (680g) are generally missing from the draft net catch. Recent work on the Killary Harbour Draft Net Fishery has shown that the average size of the eighty-six sea trout caught during the 1984 season was 16½in (42cm). The average size of the rod-caught fish in the River Erriff, at the head of the Killary, was approximately 11½in (30cm).

More recent tagging experiments have shown that the Killary Harbour fishery also includes sea trout from both the Screeb and Burrishoole fisheries. Tagged sea trout from Tawnyard Lough on the Erriff system have also been recorded from the neighbouring Delphi system.

Boosting productivity

It has been known for some time that shoals of post-smolts, in particular, move freely between neighbouring estuaries and also back and forth between fresh water and the sea. They therefore exhibit a great degree of physiological plasticity and can adapt to a wide range of different salinities over a relatively short period of time.

Since we have for so many years been thoroughly bereft of reliable quantitative information on the dynamics of our sea trout populations, it is no wonder that the fisheries authorities have found it difficult to advise on sound management strategies for our sea trout stocks. In management terms, we have improved little on the strategies and techniques which were available at the turn of the century.

However, it is axiomatic that adult sea trout numbers are directly dependent on the numbers of juvenile sea trout produced. Since sea trout often spawn in tiny mountain or forest streams, their production is more likely to be affected by such factors as field drainage, bog drainage, agricultural pollution, afforestation and deforestation. It is my own firm belief that sea trout numbers are limited by the productive potential of the spawning streams and not by the holding capacity of the parent lakes and rivers, which is normally surplus to the needs of the catchment. The maintenance and improvement of spawning and nursery areas is probably the single most important aspect of managing a sea trout fishery.

The movement, particularly of the larger sea trout in a system, is dependent on water levels.

Regulation of water discharge could be used in sea trout fisheries to create artificial spates, which would in turn generate a supply of fresh fish into the system under low water conditions. The installation of a sluice system at a lake outfall in the lower catchment could quite effectively regulate water flow. A run of fresh fish under drought conditions might not guarantee good angling but it would certainly reduce the level of draft net exploitation in the estuary and hopefully boost spawning stocks.

Hopes are also growing that the selective or genetic manipulation of sea trout stocks may lead to an overall improvement in the average size. As mentioned, finnock contribute little to the spawning stocks in most Irish fisheries and it is now becoming apparent that it is the one- and two-sea-winter maiden sea trout which should be conserved. The concept of a slot limit which would protect these maidens and leave the angler free to take finnock and 'trophy' fish is growing in acceptance. Even more exciting is the prospect that a genetic factor may be involved in choosing whether or not a fish returns as a finnock or a maiden. Selective culling of finnock may ultimately lead to an overall improvement in the average size of Irish sea trout.

A true sport fish

There is no doubt that sea trout are of far greater economic importance as a sport fish than as a commercial species. They have, for too long, been considered a poor relative of the salmon. Let us hope that the day is not far off when the true value of the sea trout will be recognised and that it will gain the legal protection of being declared a non-commercial sport fish.

Types of fishery

In Ireland there are two principal types of sea trout fishery: those where the catch is predominantly composed of sea trout, with few salmon, and those where sea trout are taken as a by-catch while salmon fishing.

The major sea trout fisheries are located in Donegal, Mayo, Connemara, Kerry and west Cork. These often consist of a series of small lakes, located in blanket-bog and joined by short canal-like rivers. The tributaries of such systems are generally small and are principally used for spawning. The lakes constitute the main nursery habitat in these systems.

In Ireland, the average size of angling-caught sea trout is small. This is due to the large numbers of post-smolts present in the catch. However, preliminary results from the Erriff fishery indicate that anglers' catches do not fully reflect the true stock of older sea trout in a system. This is mainly due to the relative movement of post-smolts and larger sea trout. Research has shown that post-smolts may ascend at any time during a twenty-four hour period, even under relatively low flow conditions. The larger sea trout only move at night, except during high water conditions. It would seem that the key factor in catching the larger fish is to concentrate angling activity into periods of peak fish movements.

The larger sea trout are equally difficult to catch in the loughs. One example from the west of Ireland will help to illustrate this point. Tawnyard Lough is a fine sea trout fishery which forms part of the Erriff system in County Mayo. During the drought of 1984, angling conditions were far from ideal and angling pressure was light. As a result, the lake only produced 108 sea trout (CPUE .658). Over 50 per cent of these fish were finnock and the remainder were between 12 and 16in (30 and 40cm). In the spring of 1985 a portion of the kelt run was trapped as part of an ongoing scientific programme and over 400 adults ranging in size from 10 to 24in (25–60cm) were recorded. Some 200 sea trout in this sample were in excess of 16in (40cm). It is obvious from these results that anglers need to adopt a radically new approach to fishing Irish sea trout loughs!

One notable exception to the above is Lough Currane, near Waterville, County Kerry. This fishery contains a long-lived strain of sea trout, a significant proportion of which become multi-spawners. These larger sea trout enter the fishery in May and June and provide excellent sport for a six- to eight-week period. Trout caught at this time may have an average weight of 2lb (1kg) and trout between 6 and 10lb (2.5–4.5 kg) are regularly taken on wet flies.

Traditional angling methods

The bulk of Irish rod-caught sea trout are taken on the fly and this method has consistently proven the most effective. Sea trout fishing is generally carried out on loughs during the hours of daylight and little experimentation has been done on developing new night fishing techniques, which might result in a more consistent harvest of the larger residents. There is little tradition of true night fishing for sea trout in Irish rivers and, although a few notable exceptions do exist (eg Ballynahinch fishery in Connemara and some of the east coast rivers), Irish anglers are largely unaware of the night fishing techniques used, with such consistent success, by their Welsh and English neighbours.

Surprisingly few sea trout are taken on the worm or while spinning. These methods are generally frowned upon except where sea trout are taken as a by-catch while salmon fishing. From my own limited experience, I know how effective both these methods can be and perhaps it is just as well that a fly-only rule exists on most of the prestigious fisheries.

I remember my first visit to a really high-class sea trout fishery many years ago. The proprietor neglected to mention the fact that the waters were fly-only and in the absence of any notice to that effect my companions and I decided to put a spinning rod in the boat — just in case. By mid-afternoon we had become totally becalmed and had not risen a fish. My dad reckoned that we should anchor the boat and fish some of the deeper gullies in the lake. My brother and I opposed this view and maintained that we should continue to search the lake for the few fleeting breezes which ruffled its surface from time to time. Eventually, Dad, in a fit of total exasperation, asked to be marooned on a large, flat-topped, granite boulder, which had obvious designs on eventually becoming an island. To add insult to injury, he declined his fly rod and took with him the spinning rod and the attached 2in (5cm) blue and silver Devon. Some thirty minutes later we returned to 'nut island', as we had affectionately named the rock, to find a very satisfied father contentedly puffing on his pipe and admiring a fine 3lb (1.5kg) sea trout. We decided that discretion was the better part of valour and on his instructions fished deep shelves, at anchor, for the remainder of the day — but not a single fish came to the fly.

Irish sea trout are also taken in bays and estuaries around the coast. Most of these fish are caught as a by-catch while spinning for mackerel or pollack. Recent experimental fishing, using mackerel strip and sandeels, has proven very successful and many large 3 to 5lb (1.5–2.5kg) fish have been taken. This is particularly true of County Donegal where the sea trout takes the place of the majestic bass in the surf beaches. Exciting fishing awaits the innovative fly angler who is prepared to develop suitable saltwater techniques.

One word of warning. When sea trout kelts re-enter the sea in April or early May, they feed ravenously and are easily taken by a variety of methods. While still in fresh water many of the males recover both condition and their typical silver coating and on entering salt water can easily be mistaken for maiden fish. However, they are of little culinary value and the angler is well advised to return all sea trout caught during these two months.

Lake fishing

Sea trout loughs

Irish sea trout loughs are generally located in areas of extensive blanket-bog along the western seaboard. These are mainly small waters, ranging in size from 5 to 200 acres (2–80 ha). If, on a clear day, one takes the time to climb some of the higher peaks surrounding these marsh and bogland expanses, the intertwining lake systems may be seen like sparkling jewels stretching off into the hazy horizon, defying individual identification. Although frequently located in mountain terrain, Irish sea trout loughs are generally no more than localised depressions in the surrounding granite or sandstone. They are shallow waters, often characterised by rock-studded margins and deeper black gullies left by the retreating glaciers. They have changed little in the intervening 10 000 years and although the peaty black water may imply great depth, the angler is ever surprised by the appearance of jagged rocks and stones which seem to vault from the lake bottom in a never-ending effort to discourage the impertinent traveller. These are spate lakes which may rise and fall a half metre or more in a twenty-four hour period. Despite their size, they are dangerous lakes where an engine is rarely used, except by experts or reckless amateurs, and where a 4in (10cm) rise or fall in water level may change completely the surface contours and the angler's drifts.

Where the deeper gullies plummet to depths of 10 or 20m, char are present. These are enigmatic, mysterious creatures, often present in fair abundance but, due to their preference for deeper water, rarely encountered by anglers. Ireland's char are part of an ancient lineage and were amongst the first salmonids to enter fresh water from the cold glacial seas. In peat-stained waters the coloration of the resident char practically defies description. If you are fortunate enough to hook one of these beautiful creatures, take time to admire the vivid orange red of the tummy, the halo of gold about the flanks, dotted with large, obtrusive black spots and the cold granite grey of the back. If you take a char, do not kill it out of curiosity or ignorance as many have done before and leave its remains to rot on the boards of the boat. Treat it with the respect it richly deserves and gently return this glacial relic to its ancestral home.

Patterns of movement

As fresh sea trout enter these lakes they invariably push onwards towards the inflow and, if conditions suit, they ascend to the lake above. However, if the inflowing stream is dropping, the fish may find themselves, having rested, confined to a particular water, and it is only then that they disperse to the more favourable lies around the margins. I always find it helpful to imagine the behaviour of my quarry as I search the margins of lakes or rivers. In the case of sea trout from the loughs, I am always tempted to believe that they have an area of residence where the shoal is most likely to be found. However, at times, the fish vacate these haunts and for some unknown reason promenade freely about the surface of the lake. It is only when in residence that fish may be consistently taken. I should mention that in the shallower lakes practically the whole surface area is worth fishing and that the lake should be fished in as near to parallel drifts as possible. In the deeper lakes it is the margins in shallow, rocky areas which are most productive.

Knowing your way around

Until you know your sea trout lake (or indeed system) really well, the advice and assistance of a good gillie is almost indispensable. For consistently good sea trout fishing is as much about boat handling as it is about good angling.

Some years ago, two friends and I spent a very frustrating few days fishing Lough Currane in County Kerry. The locals maintained that the lake was well stocked and certainly there were many fresh fish in evidence. We were students at the time and our finances would not stretch to employing a gillie, so we struggled on in our ignorance, catching one or two good-sized sea trout on each of the first three days. But two 1½lb (680g) sea trout for three rods fishing ten hours or more is certainly not good fishing. On the Sunday morning at about 11.30 am we called back into the boat quay to collect some forgotten items from the car. On the shore we met our old friend Sonny Connell from Killarney, who had first introduced us to Lough Currane. With him was his father, and his eldest son, who was, I think, about eight or nine years old at the time. They explained that they had heard the lake was fishing well and had decided to introduce the young boy to the joys of sea trout. Nothing strenuous was planned and they reckoned they would only fish two areas at most, Church Island and the Grassy — a long shallow area stretching from the point of Church Island to the mouth of the inflowing Cummeragh River.

We left them still tackling up at 12.00 pm and, having exchanged some killer patterns, we headed for the far side of the lake. We had, by our standards, quite a productive afternoon; two sea trout about 1½lb (680g) and a finnock of 10oz (280g). We also rose a number of other fish. On our return to the shore we encountered Sonny busily unloading the boat. He had promised to be home by 6.00 pm but the fishing was quite good and so he had stayed on a little longer than expected. He perfunctorily admired our catch and, when pressed, rather sheepishly announced 'Oh, we got nine'. That phrase still rings in my ears. The old oilskin was then thrown back to reveal the most magnificent bag of sea trout, ranging in size from 2 to 4lb (1-2kg). Four of the larger fish had been taken on a Watson's Fancy, which my brother had given to Sonny. The young boy then produced the bailing can which was stuffed with five or six finnock. Sonny explained that in order to give the lad some practice he had 'run over a few juner areas' late in the afternoon. The three of us almost wept with total frustration and just a hint of jealousy!

Later visits in the company of Sonny revealed his secrets; an intimate knowledge of the bottom contours and the ability to manoeuvre a boat constantly in the desired direction. Not for him the long, easy drift but rather the constant, hard pull and push of the oars and the constant re-positioning of the boat. Whenever I am tempted to take a long, easy drift on a sea trout lough, that phrase of 'Oh, we got nine', rings in my ears. A salutary lesson indeed.

Rudders, leeboards and drogues

In recent years some of the more innovative reservoir anglers from the English midlands have taken to adopting old mariner and barge captain tactics to regulate and control the direction and speed of their boats. They have re-invented the wheel to some extent by introducing a whole new generation to the advantages of using rudders, leeboards and most importantly of all, drogues. Using a combination of both rudder and leeboard, you can fish chosen tracts of water rather than traditional,

wind-defined drifts. By re-positioning the boat's occupants you can maximise your efficiency and the area fished. All details regarding the use of these devices may be found in Bob Church's excellent book *Reservoir Trout Fishing*.

Although the use of leeboards and rudders has great potential in Irish sea trout fishing, there is one major disadvantage — their weight. In situations where one has to track across a kilometre or more of wild bogland before reaching one's boat, it would be a mighty man indeed that could include a rudder and a set of leeboards and clamps in his back pack! However, where boats are readily accessible the regular angler could, with some practice and experimentation, greatly improve

63

his ability to consistently fish the more productive water.

The drogue is probably the sea trout angler's most important ancillary device. It is basically a 1 metre square piece of nylon or pvc which is tied by the four corners to a large swivel. This in turn is attached to a 2 or 3m thin nylon rope. Because of its light construction it adds little to the weight of a back pack. The further astern the drogue is set, the harder it bites and the more it curtails the speed of the boat. Drogues are particularly useful in situations where engines are not permitted, for a strong wind can make fishing in such situations almost impossible. Having taken twenty to thirty minutes to row up to the top of your chosen drift, you will find, in the absence of a drogue, that it only takes four or five minutes for the wind to sweep you back to your starting point. Rushing along at such speed you have little chance to fish effectively.

In really strong winds (force 7 or more) drogues can be dangerous and should only be used by experienced anglers. They may also become fouled in sub-surface obstacles such as rocks, boulders, old tree trunks, etc, and if any real difficulty arises it is as well to have a sharp knife to hand and simply to cut the leader rope. Light nylon ropes are semi-buoyant and if brightly coloured can easily be seen, even in the darkest waters. It is far better to lose a relatively inexpensive drogue than to risk a serious accident.

Favourable conditions

The best time to fish these sea trout loughs is generally late morning (from 11.00 am to 1.30 pm), and late afternoon to early evening (from 4.00 pm to 8.00 pm). However, never make the mistake of abandoning the lake when the fish are still moving, for they can suddenly go off the take and become dour and unresponsive. I have also noticed with resident sea trout that, although they are not strictly-speaking feeding fish, they rarely ignore an easy meal and a large fall of ants or the arrival of hordes of daddy-long-legs on the surface may stimulate their latent appetite and result in a most fruitful period of surface activity.

The ideal sea trout weather is a combination of sunshine and showers, moderate temperatures, flashes of sunshine and a moderate to fresh force 4 to 5 west/south-west wind. The presence of fresh run sea trout and a settled lake complete the picture. Sea trout dislike extremes of any kind and the worst possible conditions are a rapidly rising lake, a drought-ridden lake with surface temperatures over 15°C, or electrical storms. Under ideal conditions, lake angling can be a very effective way to exploit the sea trout stock. In some years upwards of a fifth of the stock may be taken by anglers; however, it is more usual for them to take some 10 or 12 per cent.

EQUIPMENT

Fly rods

Standard tackle for Irish loughs consists of an 11ft (3.5m) carbon fibre rod which may take a size 6-8 double-tapered fly line. In recent years I have largely abandoned the use of floating lines when sea trout fishing, in favour of a sink-tip or slow-sinking line.

For bank fishing I would recommend a stiff action 9½-10½ft (3m) reservoir-type rod, capable of taking a size 8-10 forward-tapered floating or sink-tip line. I find such tackle particularly useful for lure fishing.

For night fishing in a river, a standard 9ft (2.5m) river rod is normally all that is required. However, if you intend to fish large lures you will find that the reservoir rod has many advantages over the softer-action river rod.

Fly reels

These vary in diameter from 3 to 3½in (7.5-9cm) but are generally of the wide spool variety. They should be loaded with some 80-100m of braided nylon backing, for the majority of sea trout loughs also hold grilse and the occasional summer salmon. A strong ratchet and conveniently located drag control are also essential.

Lines

The line must match the rod but a size 7 double-tapered line is considered an ideal all-round choice. However, when night fishing, there are great advantages to be gained from carrying a range of lines of different densities.

Leaders (casts)

I prefer a tapered cast even when wet-fly fishing. This is generally composed of: 1½ft of 20lb, 6-8ft of 12lb and 3-5ft of 8lb (45cm of 9kg, 1.5-2.5m of 5.5kg, 1-1.5m of 3.5kg). When boat fishing I use either one or two droppers, but when shore fishing I never use more than one dropper. Droppers should stand out from the cast and should be 4-6in (10-15cm) long. I use lighter casts only when conditions demand it and rarely, if ever, use less than 4lb (2kg) nylon when lake fishing. When night fishing I use a single fly or lure. The strength of the leader is of course varied, depending on the size and weight of lure being fished.

Net

For boat fishing use a round 18-24in (45-60cm) net with a long 3-3½ft (1m) handle. For shore fishing use a 16in (40cm) diameter round net with a light frame and light 1m handle. Either plug the handle with a cork or attach a floating lanyard to the net. This will ensure that the net can be placed beside you when wading but that either the handle or the lanyard will float.

Footwear

There is no need for waders when boat fishing — wellington boots are adequate. When shore fishing use waders or, in areas which are well known to you, body waders.

Flies

When choosing sea trout patterns, one need go no further than the advice of Kingsmill-Moore:

Flies? There are innumerable patterns from which to choose and plenty of scope for personal preferences. Provided that the size is correct and certain general principles kept in mind the exact pattern is not of such very great importance.

White trout flies should be dressed on a hook with a wide gape, so as to take as big a grip as possible. A wide gape means that there is increased leverage at the bend, and therefore the wire of the hook should be extra strong. White trout prefer a compact, chunky, thick-set body, the antithesis of the slinky type of fly used for greased-line salmon fishing. Fish winged flies at the tail, and hackle or bumble patterns on the droppers. Choose dark colours rather than light, rich colours rather than gaudy, rough bodies in preference to smooth.

The fish do seem to single out particular colours on certain days and in certain places, and the factors which govern their choice appear to be the nature of the bottom, the light, the kind of sky, the colour of the water and the length of time that has elapsed since the fish left the sea.

The three most important colours in sea trout flies are black, claret and blue. In particularly dark or peat-stained water, silver and orange may also have a role to play.

Finally I should mention those most horrific inhabitants of our sea trout loughs, the biting midges. The paucity of mammalian blood donors in these barren lands seems to instil into these tiny creatures a ferocity and a tenacity which is difficult to describe. An exposed surface vein is gladly shared and the rate of blood extraction would do justice to medicinal leeches. Before venturing out of the car, cover your face, neck and hands with a liberal coating of midge repellent (Fly-Pel is my own favourite) and remember to bring the tube with you to the lake, for perspiration quickly dissolves the best of creams or sprays. In the words of one of my companions: 'Swat. These bloody ... swat ... yokes ... swat ... could eat ... swat ... an elephant!'

SEA TROUT FISHING TECHNIQUES

The month-long drought in August left the lake a tepid, lifeless shadow of its former self; the once submerged rocks and stones protruding from its side like the bare bones of an ageing corpse. On my last visit, the only evidence of fish had been the slow roll of a large red salmon which cruised about aimlessly over the fine sandbar at the mouth of the inflowing stream. September brought the rains and a full twenty-four hour downpour which filled the system with renewed life and hope. Fresh harvesters and maidens poured into the lakes as the flood receded, and accompanied by those fish which had entered in late June and July, they had forged their way high into the hills.

As a consequence the fishing was superb and boats averaged fifteen to twenty sea trout a day. Connemara sea trout are small and a bag of around ten fish would normally contain five or six finnock and a range of larger fish between 1½ and 3lb (0.5 and 1.5kg) in weight.

It is now ten days since that initial large flood and, despite a small secondary flood three days previously, the lake which we are to fish has settled and the water has cleared. My companion for the day is a local angler, Tom Benett, whose experience and knowledge of the system should ensure a better than average chance of a successful day.

Our lake is Lugeen on the Invermore system. It is some 80 acres (30ha) in extent and lies between the bottom lough on the system, Lough Invermore, and the legendary Lough Curreel, which is about 3km further inland. Lugeen is joined by a narrow neck of water to Little Lugeen which is no more than a large river pool. It is rather a deep little adjunct and the area near its inflowing stream can often produce a grilse or two. In contrast to the remainder of the Inver system, outboard engines are permitted on Lugeen but they are only used when travelling through the centre of the lake and most experienced anglers avoid their use near the butts or the general shoreline.

Tom has advised that I should fish three flies and a sink-tip line: a size 8 Claret Bumble for the top dropper, a small (size 10) Fox and Orange for the middle, and a short, chunky size 10 Watson's Fancy for the tail. He himself has chosen a size 8 Green Peter for the top dropper followed by a size 10 Dunkeld and a size 10 Black Pennell. I also assemble my reservoir rod, for Lugeen can at times fish very well from the shore, and I place a size 8 forward-tapered, slow-sinking line with a size 8 long-shanked Appetizer on the tail and a smaller size 10 silver Muddler on the top dropper. Tom looks rather discouragingly at the reservoir tackle — he has little time for such 'nonsense'.

We motor up through the centre of the lake towards the butts and Tom cuts the engine with 100m to go. On my request he rows me to the shore some 30m above the inflowing river. Lugeen lies roughly on an east-west axis and the west/south-west wind is blowing directly towards where I have landed. Tom moves off gently, easing the boat out towards a belt of reeds at the very point of the lake. Despite twenty minutes of hard, concentrated fishing, neither Tom nor I manage to move a trout. Back in the boat we decide to try a long drift down the long axis of the lake, but hugging close to the southern shore. We clamp two leeboards onto the starboard side of the boat and gently move along, about two to three boat lengths out from the shore. Lugeen is deeper than the average sea trout lough in Ireland, with a particularly steep gradient along the mid section of the northern shore. Most anglers avoid this area, but my best Lugeen sea trout (3lb+; 1.5kg) came from here. However, for the present our attention is focused along the southern shore.

After about ten minutes there is a vicious splash at my top dropper and a sudden lunge as the hooked fish takes to the air. Following a most spectacular display of aerobatics, I net a beautifully fresh sea trout of 1¼lb (570g); the Claret Bumble is set firmly in the scissors. While I am removing the fly, Tom hooks a much larger fish which does not show but stays deep and plays strong and dour, much like a large brown trout. The fish comes loose before we have a chance to see him. For the next half an hour we meet groups of taking fish along the drift and almost invariably one or two rises are followed by a blank period and then a repeat performance in another location. Despite our best efforts, we only manage to hook and land two rather small finnock of 10 or 11oz (300g). One of these is very coloured after a prolonged stay in fresh water and Tom returns him to the water. Just before lunch the fish cease to take and we spend a fruitless thirty minutes or so fishing the shallows at the eastern end of the lake.

During lunch I convince Tom that a drift along the northern shore could prove interesting. By this time the wind has gone around to the west and strengthened to force 6. We attach the drogue to the stern and set the boat on a drift parallel to the shore. When fishing along the wind, it is best to have the two anglers facing in opposite directions. I choose to fish towards the centre of the lake while Tom fishes towards the shore. There is little point in fishing my sink-tip in the deep water and so I opt for my reservoir rod and a slow-sinking line. I will be fishing the shelf and by casting some 20 or 25m from the boat and letting it sink, the boat itself will draw the sinking line along.

A short time after starting our drift, my line suddenly stops and tightens. At first all my instincts tell me it is a grilse, but suddenly, far off the stern of the boat, a fine sea trout jumps and my line jerks in response. The boat was travelling more slowly than I had allowed for and a large belly had developed in the sinking line. The sea trout had taken the lure as it turned to follow the line of the

boat and my line had only transmitted the resistance several seconds after it had occurred. By this time the disgruntled fish was heading for the surface.

My trout gives an excellent account of itself and combines all that is best in aerial display and deep, dogged burrowing. Finally, my 2½lb (1kg) trout is in the boat. A surprisingly plump fish, it is bright silver with sea lice attached to its flank and tail.

We are disappointed with the remainder of the drift, for despite ideal conditions we only manage to land several small brown trout which are carefully unhooked and returned to the water. Tom suggests a drift in Little Lugeen, for it often fishes well in a good strong wind. As we make our way towards the arch of the bridge which divides the two lakes, I see a large fish pitch in the small lake below. We move into position just below the bridge and drift along the northern shore which leads to the butts of Little Lugeen. As we near the area where the fish moved, Tom's line streaks out into the centre of the lake and a very large sea trout takes to the air. The fish really puts on a display of strength, but after five or six minutes it is ready for the net. When we finally get it on board, we are both amazed at the ugliness of the creature. It is dark, almost black in coloration, but the body is still rotund and strong-looking. It has a large ugly kype and a great, flat, wedged-shaped tail. It had taken the Dunkeld, a common enough occurrence in September when the male sea trout become aggressive and will often attack a fly containing bright red, claret, or best of all, orange. Tom decides that there is little point in killing the fish since the flesh would be almost tasteless and so he gently eases the four-pound-plus fish over the gunwale.

We row the boat back upwind towards the bridge and begin a second drift along the northern shore towards the inflowing stream. As we near the slow, soft eddy which lies at the edge of the current, a small grilse gives a beautiful head and tail rise. I cast my team of flies into the fast-moving current and draw them enticingly across the eddy. There is a strong boil and splash. I instinctively lift the rod and to my surprise the line streaks out across the current. Had it been the salmon which took my dropper I would surely have lost it, for my reactions were far too fast. My 'salmon' turns out to be a fine maiden sea trout of 1¼lb (570g).

By now the evening is drawing in and the sun has set over the Connemara coastline. We make our way back to the local hostelry for a pint and a chat, well satisfied with our day's catch of six sea trout. Not a record day by any means, but we had fished hard and received our just rewards.

River fishing

Distinct behavioural patterns

Tackling river sea trout is a completely different prospect. These are normally fresh run, highly sensitive creatures, ready to react to any disturbance and aware of the least change in oxygen concentration or barometric pressure. The larger adults sneak through the fishery at night, often undetected, while the smaller finnock are more foolhardy and may be seen moving through flows and riffles by day. The movements of river sea trout are not confined to periods of high water and nocturnal movements may take place even under relatively low flow conditions. The fortunate angler may, as I have done myself on several occasions, witness a mass movement of finnock around dawn. On one such occasion the fish moved up a shallow, gravelly run in such numbers that, at times, they were sliding along the sides of my boots. They refused to take anything I offered them and seemed solely interested in forging further upstream. It is thought that sea trout do not normally move great distances in any twenty-four hour period and discrete shoals of fish may be monitored from pool to pool by the observant angler. Under low water conditions, the lower pools in a fishery may hold exceptionally large numbers of fish and it is quite a common fault to assume the whole river is equally well stocked. However, it must be remembered that under prolonged drought conditions, 80 per cent or more of the potential spawning stock of a system may be concentrated into these lower pools.

In the sea, these trout are active predators and when they first enter fresh water a high proportion may retain this acquired behaviour. Anglers new to sea trout often restrict themselves to small flies in the mistaken opinion that they will behave in a similar way to brown trout. Nothing could be further from the truth. Even finnock will actively chase long, bright, sub-surface lures. My favourite 'fly' for day-time finnock fishing is a long-shanked size 10 silver Muddler. It is particularly effective where a portion of the shoal is lying at the edge of fast water near the neck of the pool.

69

Night fishing

River fishing for the larger sea trout is primarily a night-time exercise. Fishing in the pitch dark along heavily treed rivers when your only companions are the rumblings of the night, bats and rats, is not everyone's idea of fun. Yet the excitement of the unseen take, the plops and splashes of moving fish, the heightening of the tactile and auditory senses all combine to provide a uniquely thrilling experience. If you are a night fisher by nature, few other angling pleasures can compare with or replace its attractions.

Falkus, the doyen of night fishing for sea trout, has defined concentration, confidence, stealth and persistence as the key elements in successful night fishing. In my experience these must be combined with detailed reconnaissance and careful planning. It is also important to confine your activities to one or at most two pools and to pick your companions very, very carefully. To quote Falkus, one should avoid those companions whose concept of sea trout fishing is 'A jolly prattle with his friends over a midnight barbecue'. My choice of companion would be someone who, having become over-adventurous and lost his footing, would noiselessly float by whispering 'Psst ...Psst ... I think I am drowning'! With a really good companion it is possible to communicate almost without words.

Night fishing may be divided into three phases, dusk to midnight, midnight to 1 am, and 1 am to daylight. Falkus has named these periods as first half, half-time and second half, respectively. The most productive of these three periods is the first half. One of the most difficult decisions to make when night fishing is when exactly the first half begins. On a bright moonlit night it may be 11.00 pm or later before one dares to approach the edge of the chosen pool. However, on dark, damp evenings one may be fishing before 10.30 pm. Sea trout behaviour changes completely once darkness has fallen and the shy, retiring creature which furtively darted from one corner of the pool to the other during daylight may now move without fear into the shallows at the tail of the pool or lie in the faster water at its neck. River sea trout prefer slow, deep pools — the 'flats' of the brown trout fisherman — the complete antithesis of the fast, strong currents one would imagine to be an ideal habitat for such a strong, lithe, streamlined creature.

Different approaches

If water temperatures are average or a little above, the first half is normally devoted to either the floating line or the sink-tip. I must confess that I rarely bother with the floating line for sea trout and concentrate all my efforts on either the sink-tip or sinking line. I normally fish only one fly at night as I know from experience how a tangle of two or three flies can be fished unnoticed for an hour or more. Landing a large sea trout at night whilst trailing a dropper or two is, in my opinion, a foolhardy business and normally results in a broken cast and a lost fish. Worse still, the fish is left to trail several feet of nylon about for days until it manages to throw the hook. The sea trout angler should not be afraid to fish quite large lures or flies, even during the first half; probably the most consistently efficient fly at this time is a size 6 or 8 Medicine. Stale or potted sea trout behave more like salmon and they may be inclined to take a smaller, more traditional fly.

As we move into half-time or the second half, it may be necessary to locate the sea trout near the bottom of the pool, as dropping temperatures may make them reticent to take near the surface. A change is then required to a sinking line. The choice of slow, medium or fast sinking is really defined by the nature and depth of the pool being fished. In most cases a medium line is ideal. The lures (for it is mainly lures one fishes at this time) are fished near the bottom and retrieved very, very slowly. Please remember that fishing a heavy lure on a floating or sink-tip line will result in the lure fishing relatively high in the water. To fish consistently deep, a sinking line is essential.

Some years ago I had the good fortune to fish the Dovey in Wales for several evenings in the company of Graeme Harris (author of *Successful Sea Trout Angling*). Graeme is a very experienced sea trout angler and it was quite a treat to see how, under the most unfavourable conditions, he could winkle out fine sea trout up to 4lb (2kg) in weight from the drought-ridden pools. His secret was that, like Sonny Connell on Lough Currane, he knew every inch of the pools he was fishing, where the fish were most likely to lie, and more importantly, where they were most likely to take. It was the nearest thing to spring salmon fishing in the dark I had ever experienced. He fished a standard 9ft (2.5m) fly rod but had a range of five or six different lines, from floaters through neutral densities to fast sinkers. He fished salmon tube flies of his own tying on 10lb (4.5kg) nylon. If he will forgive me for saying so, they were far from elegantly tied, but they were effective. My own flies were more neatly tied but were rejected out of hand by the Welsh sea trout or *sewin*. On reflection it was probably not the flies that made the difference but the depth and speed at which they were fished.

Another very effective technique during the second half is the floating lure. This works particularly well on warm evenings when the fish have gone off the take but where the presence of a large fish is suspected. A range of cork or plastic lures may be used but my own favourite is a long-shanked size 6 Muddler, well coated in floatant and fished on a floating line.

I developed this technique in the early seventies while working in Kenmare, County Kerry. Some locals and I were regularly fishing the lower pools of the Roughty River. However, in the first week's fishing I had only taken three or four sea trout while they were catching eight to ten fish each evening. I was using a 9ft (2.5m) trout rod and floating line while they were using spinning rods and bubble floats. I must admit that I was sorely tempted to use a bubble until one evening I actually saw, at dusk, a fresh sea trout chase and splash at the bubble and not the attached flies! The secret lay in the bubble's wake. The following evening I fished with a purpose-tied, floating Muddler and caught twelve sea trout and a beautifully golden 2lb (1kg) slob trout. I never looked back after that.

The night angler is particularly dependent on ancillary equipment and Falkus recommends a mnemonic to remind him of his requirements: 'RR, NN, MM, SS, F, T and P' (rods, reels, net, nylon, midge-repellent, maggots, scissors, spectacles, fly-case, torch and priest).

Maggots

The angler who is new to sea trout may find it strange that maggots should appear on the list of any self-respecting fly-fisherman. However, there are times when a maggot or two attached to a fly can prove very attractive to sea trout and it is something of a tradition in both Ireland and Britain to carry a small box of maggots with you when sea trout fishing. But remember, many fisheries are strictly fly only and maggots are prohibited. In recent years maggots have become freely available for coarse fishing. Their use has been much abused, particularly in ground baiting for brown and sea trout. The use of ground bait in salmonid fisheries is an abomination and should be banned. There is a world of difference between the selective use of single or twinned maggots on a lure for sea trout and their extensive use on float or leger tackle. Coarse anglers return their catch to the water unharmed and so no holds are barred with regard to bait or ground bait. Salmonid anglers normally kill their catch, and unlimited use of coarse fishing techniques soon depletes stocks of trout in a fishery.

SEA TROUT FISHING TECHNIQUES

It is a balmy, warm summer's evening in late July and my brother and I have been invited to fish a private stretch of the River Dargle, which lies about 25km south of Dublin on Ireland's east coast. Because of its proximity to the city centre and the popular seaside resort of Bray, the Dargle suffers more than its fair share of poaching, despite the best efforts of the water keepers. Gangs of poachers regularly visit the fishery, but it is a credit to its productivity that it still maintains a good head of sea trout up to 6lb (2.5kg) or more. Many years ago there was a problem with poison but thankfully that seems to have died out. It is difficult to denude a fishery of its total stock by intermittent poaching but poisoning disrupts the whole food chain within a river and may wipe out several generations of fish in a few short minutes.

Having arrived at 9.30 pm we have at least an hour to wait before starting to fish. A quick and careful reconnaissance along the bank (keeping back some 20 or 30m) has revealed several fresh fish jumping and so we are confident that there are still fish in the pools. Our host had assured us that a flood two days previously had brought up a good head of fresh fish, and some sea trout of between 2 and 4lb (1–2kg) were taken.

We tackle up. I am using a standard 9ft (2.5m) fly rod, a size 6 sink-tip line and a single size 8 Medicine on the point. Brendan is using a similar fly rod but has opted for a slow-sinking line and two flies: a size 10 Black Pennell on the dropper and a size 8 Dunkeld on the point.

We have available to us two consecutive pools leading into a deep, fast, rocky run. I choose the middle pool while Brendan decides to fish the lower run. The larger, top pool, is left undisturbed until it is really dark.

I cast my fly across the pool at an angle of approximately 75°, let the fly sink for a few seconds and begin a rather smart retrieve. I am a great believer in altering the rate and depth of retrieve for sea trout and I constantly change the pace of the line and the depth of the fly. When attached to a floating or sink-tip line the fly should ideally be fished at a depth of 4 to 12in (10 to 30cm) and I would suggest that this is the ideal depth range for the first half.

Almost immediately there is a sharp tug and my heart leaps. But it is only a plump 9in (25cm) brown trout. I wet my hand and unhook the fish, returning it carefully to the water. Sea trout smolts of four or five years of age are not uncommon and it is best to treat all brown trout as potential sea trout and to return them to the water alive.

Water levels are lower than I expected and after ten minutes I decide to change to a smaller black lure tied on a long-shanked size 10 hook. Some five minutes later there is a splash well out in the centre of the pool and I am fast into my first Dargle sea trout. The fight is fast and furious and I am convinced that I have hooked a really good fish. When the 1¼lb (570g) trout is finally in the net I am rather disappointed; the darkness and strength of the fish had belied its true weight. This often happens when sea trout fishing, and anglers should not be too quick to guess the weight of their catch until it is firmly on the bank.

As I move back to fish the pool, Brendan beckons me from below. I join him and find that the rising tide has brought fresh finnock which are splashing through the shallows up into the deep run. He has already taken one plump ¾lb (340g) finnock and hooked two others. The mouths of fresh sea trout are soft and hooks pull out easily. There are two opposing schools of thought on how to deal with this problem. One recommends that you hold against the jumping fish and not drop your rod tip; it is claimed that this will sink home the hook. The alternative and quite contradictory view is that the rod tip should be dropped as the fish jumps. In my experience, to hold against the fish is to court disaster.

During the next twenty hectic minutes we take five nice finnock and lose as many more. Then almost as suddenly as the run had started, the fish are gone. It is now 11.30 and we have done very well; our total bag is five finnock and one maiden.

Having taken a short rest we decide it is time to hunt for a really large fish in the top pool. Brendan wades across to fish the neck of the pool, which is unfishable from the near bank, and I content myself with the middle and tail of the pool. I change to a slow-sinking line and replace my black lure with a long tandem blue and silver lure. Brendan has changed to a size 6 Medicine.

The darkness and the soft rustle of the trees seem in complete harmony with the low 'swish, swish' of the lines as they are fed and retrieved through the rod rings. My reverie is broken by a great heave and splash down at the tail of the pool. A sharp 'Ken' from the far bank indicates that Brendan has also heard the splash. No more need be said. I leave the fish to settle and after a few minutes slowly fish my way back towards the tail of the pool.

As I move downstream I recall a similar incident on the River Erriff when the 'fish', having splashed, continued to swim up the pool towards me. I was so convinced that the huge bow wave was made by a salmon that I cast frantically at the dimly lit furrow. After about five quite accurate casts, a greatly irritated dog otter surfaced near to me. He looked me straight between the eyes, wrinkled his great whiskers in annoyance and disappeared once again into 'my' pool. I retired to the river's edge and sat quietly on a large stone. Despite my obvious presence, the otter continued to fish for a further ten or fifteen minutes. At least three times he surfaced near to the rock, as if to check that my intentions were honourable, and then resumed his business. Such an experience adds immeasurably to the thrills of fishing by night.

Having fished to the tail of the pool without success, I change to a floating line and tie on a bushy size 6, long-shanked Muddler. I move back up the pool and retrace my steps towards the tail. In addition to the wake, the head of the Muddler also makes a loud plopping noise as I retrieve it across the pool. As it nears the shallow lip of the pool there is a violent splash and a frantic lurch as the rod buckles in my hand. Line screeches from the reel as the fish wallows and dashes through the shallow water up into the deeper pool. By this stage it is obvious to everyone within earshot that I am fast in a large fish, and, abandoning his usual calm ways, Brendan dashes across the tail of the pool to my assistance. Initially the fish gives a most dramatic display of acrobatics but eventually adopts a pattern of deep, powerful runs. Brendan has both torch and long-handled net at the ready. After three or four heart-pounding minutes, the fish is ready to be netted. As he lowers the net, Brendan switches on the torch and lifts the fish cleanly onto the bank. It is a fine 3 lb+ (1.5kg) fish, fresh from the sea, with a row of egg-laden sea lice along its back and tail. The fish is quickly dispatched.

It is now 12.30 am and we decide that the commotion and lights have put pay to our chances of further sport. But we are well satisfied as we make our way towards the car.

Alternative angling methods

Sea trout fishing methods other than fly fishing are generally reserved for periods of either extreme high or extreme low water. These methods should be used sparingly, with an eye to conservation, good sportsmanship and the rights of other anglers. It is fortunate that in sea trout fishing there is generally a clear distinction between those times when fish may be attracted to the fly and periods when fly fishing is both out of the question technically and singularly unsuccessful. On most Irish sea trout lakes anglers are restricted to a fly-only rule and I will therefore concentrate exclusively on river fishing in the following section.

Bubble float

A bubble float is a clear, hollow, plastic float ranging from about 1 to 3in (2.5-7.5cm) in diameter. It has two small plastic bungs inserted in its side and by removing these and immersing the float under water, the entrapped air is released and the desired level of water may be allowed into the float. It is normal to three-quarters fill the float and then to re-insert the stoppers. There is a metal-coated eye on both the top and the bottom of the float and these are used when attaching the float to the main line.

When used for 'fly' fishing, two droppers are normally placed some 18-30in (45-75cm) above the float and a tail of 12-14in (30-35cm) is left behind the bubble. The advantage of the bubble technique is that it may be used by the relatively inexperienced fly-fisherman who has a good knowledge of spinning tackle. The bubble is generally fished on a standard 6-8ft (2-2.5m) spinning rod, with a fixed-spool reel containing 6-10lb (2.5-4.5kg) nylon.

It can, at times, be a very effective method, both on rivers and on lakes. The weight of the water contained in the float means that a competent angler can fish large areas of water, since up to 50m may be covered with each cast. The wake from the bubble actually attracts the sea trout and they then pounce on one of the attached flies. Please check before adopting this technique on any new water which you are fishing as it is not normally permitted in waters where the 'fly-only' rule applies.

Spinning

Spinning for sea trout can be very effective at times, particularly when fresh fish are running in very high water conditions. The standard trace I use is that shown for grilse fishing, and the normal spinners that I use are blue and silver Devons (1-2in; 2.5-5cm), Quill Minnows (1-2in; 2.5-5cm), copper and silver Tobys (¼-⅜oz; 7-12g) and Mepps (sizes 0, 1 and 2) in a variety of colours. If I were confined to two baits I would choose, without hesitation, a 7g silver Toby and a size 1 silver and copper Mepps. The addition of lead is dependent on the water level, but under dropping water conditions a ¼–½oz (7–14g) barrel lead ensures that the bait fishes 12–16in (30–40cm) below the surface, where it is most effective. Sea trout love a flashing, fast-moving bait and for that reason the direction and speed of the lure should be constantly changed. Some patterns are consistently successful. For example, a silver Toby can prove deadly if fished in a fast sink-and-draw motion.

Locating sea trout in flood waters may prove difficult, for often their high water lies are far less obvious than their low water haunts. However, if you carefully fish under your own bank, along rock ledges and in eddies and backwaters, you will eventually locate the fish. Although they are less shy under these conditions, it is as well to give hooked fish plenty of opportunity to move out into the main current and to land them well below the 'hotspot', for such small areas may hold a considerable number of sea trout in a very confined space. Adopting this technique I once landed twelve sea trout in thirty minutes from one small backwater. It was literally a case of a fish a cast until a 6lb (2.5kg) grilse grabbed the spinner and decided to thrash about near the bank for three or four minutes before it was finally landed.

If you know your river really well, a size 0 Mepps may be used to great effect under low water conditions. Choose a pool where there is heavy tree cover and where the shoal of fish is confined to a heavily shaded area along the far shelving bank. Using a short 5–6ft (1.5–2m) spinning rod, a fixed-spool reel with 4–6lb (2–3kg) nylon and as little extra weight as possible, gently cast the spinner into gaps in the trees; or if you are really expert, under the overhanging branches. Spin the Mepps as fast as possible back towards your bank. You will be amazed at the number of fish which will give chase. If your fish chase but refuse to take, stop the spinner dead in its tracks just as it reaches the edge of the shelf. As it flutters towards the bottom, one of the more adventurous fish will often grab the bait. I have even had fish pick the spinner up from the bottom as it settled.

Worming

When the river is running bank-high and the water is yellow or black, worming for sea trout is quite a simple matter. Replace your fly cast with a 9–10ft (2.5–3m) length of 10lb (4.5kg) nylon, slip on a barrel lead or bullet and place a split-shot some 18in (45cm) above a size 8 hook. A lobworm or large blackhead is placed on the hook and it is then lowered into likely looking holding areas along the edge of the bank. A firm 'knock knock' normally indicates a sea trout, but wait until the fish moves off before lifting the rod top and tightening. Remember, if the bait stops, do nothing, for it may be a grilse or a salmon and they are much slower to take a worm fully in their mouths.

Stret-pegging is also useful when sea trout fishing. This is basically a laying-on technique, where the bait is set 18in (45cm) or so deeper than the known depth of the bottom. The float is then cast and allowed to settle. Every few minutes the float's position is changed by lifting the rod tip

and allowing the bait to float several yards downstream. The top is then dropped and the float is permitted to settle. This is a most skilful form of fishing and its main advantage is its manoeuvrability. However, its use is confined to sections where the bottom is free of snags and is composed of clean sand or gravel.

Perhaps the most skilful method of worm fishing is upstream worming under low water conditions. When temperatures rise and water levels drop, both salmon and sea trout may be forced into cooler, well-oxygenated lies in runs and riffles. Rocky, fast runs some 4–6ft (1–2m) deep are ideal for the upstream worm. If at all possible, fish from the bank and avoid causing any disturbance. Cast across and upstream at an angle of 30 to 40° and allow the worm to tumble down in as natural a way as possible. A multi-hook Stewart or Pennel tackle is normally used. The worm is cast across a known lie so that the bait has settled long before reaching the desired area. Classically, upstream worming is carried out using a long fly rod and a fly reel containing stiff nylon (12–16lb; 5.5–7kg) or a smooth fly line. The cast is 6–10lb (2.5–4.5kg) nylon, depending on conditions. The only lead used is some small beads of split-shot 10 or 12in (25–30cm) above the bait. Even this may be dispensed with under really low water conditions. A long, supple spinning rod may be used in place of the fly rod. To cast, several yards of line are stripped from the reel; these are coiled on the bank and the worm is then flicked out towards the desired point in the stream.

Choosing worms
I normally fish lobworms or black-headed worms under high water conditions and small redworms or brandlings in low or medium water. However, sea trout are not as fastidious as salmon and the correct presentation is infinitely more important than the species of worm used.

Dapping

Ireland's lakes are generally windswept and shallow and as a result a strong tradition of 'dapping' has developed on these waters. Dapping in its purest form involves the use of natural insects, fished either singly or in pairs. The equipment used is a long, light, 14–16ft (4–5m) dapping rod and a fly reel with 80 to 100m of 8–10lb (3.5–4.5kg) nylon. To this is attached some 2m of extremely light but strong floss line or blow line. (Avoid floss silk at all costs as, when wet, it clings doggedly to both the rod and the rings; floss nylon is, however, ideal.) The cast consists of 4–6ft (1–2m) of 6–8lb (2.5–3.5kg) nylon and a size 8 hook. Purpose-made dapping hooks are available, but I have found these to be unreliable both from the point of view of hooking fish and the strength of the metal used. There are now some excellent light bait hooks available.

Dapping with natural insects
For sea trout fishing, the natural insects used include daddy-long-legs, grasshoppers and some of the larger heather beetles. The insects are normally attached to the hook through the thorax and the blow line is then lifted high in the air by raising the rod tip. Line is drawn from the reel and the desired length of line is allowed to billow out. When some 6 to 8m is blowing in the breeze, the rod tip is lowered until the dap touches the surface of the water. Ideally, the line and cast should remain airborne. The dap is then gently moved across the waves, leaving a most attractive furrow in its wake.

Sea trout will normally chase the dap for a short while before finally taking the insect. If you find fish rather reluctant to take the moving dap, drop your rod point when you see a movement in the wave. This will have the effect of slowing down the speed of the dap and very often results in a firm take. The fish will normally give a classic head and tail rise. Do not strike but allow it time to move down with the bait before lifting the rod tip. Be prepared for a strong response, particularly if it is a big fish, for remember you are pulling against the momentum of a diving fish. It is impossible to indicate exactly how long to wait before responding but four seconds is rarely too long.

Collecting natural insects involves either a nominal payment to the local collector of such items (invariably a small boy who just happens to be around the boat quay!) or collecting insects oneself from the lakeshore. Daddy-long-legs and beetles are to be found amongst the heathers and bracken, particularly in mid to late September. Their collection is much simplified by the use of a long-handled butterfly net. Collecting grasshoppers involves the location of an area of rough scrub grass which has not been cultivated or fertilised and the adoption of a peculiar gait affectionately named the grasshopper shuffle. The slightly stooped angler moves slowly through the grass, shuffling his feet and listening for the characteristic stridulation of a hopper. Having disturbed the insect, the observant angler notes the grasshopper's point of landing and pounces. It's not as easy as it seems and young supple reflexes are a great advantage.

Dapping with artificial flies
Artificial flies may also be used for dapping. These are normally great bushy concoctions that ride high on the surface of the water and are easily seen by both fish and angler. In recent years there has been a move away from the traditional dapping rod, particularly when using artificials, and many anglers now use a 10ft+ (3m) fly rod and a floating line or monofilament with a blow line attached. A good floatant is essential for even the most buoyant of artificials and it is hard to beat the modern silicone dressings.

A sea trout will reject an artificial faster than he will reject the natural dap. Therefore the angler must strike immediately a fish rises, particularly if he makes a great slash at the fly. If the sea trout takes a stationary fly, wait until the nylon has disappeared down the centre of the boil before lifting the rod tip. On really windy days an 'anchor fly' is often attached some sixty centimetres below the dap. This acts as a stabiliser and ensures that the larger fly does not skim uncontrollably across the surface; a size 12 Wickham's is ideal for this purpose.

Sea trout in salt water

Location
Traditionally, fishing for sea trout in salt water in Ireland has been confined to four principal locations: Garinish Island, off Glengarriff, County Kerry; Rosses Point, County Sligo; the estuaries of the Moy at Ballina, County Mayo, and of the Erne at Ballyshannon, County Donegal. In these areas the fish are mainly taken on silver spinners of various designs and little serious effort has been

made to establish a tradition of fly fishing for these trout.

Feeding sea trout abound in bays and estuaries throughout Ireland and there is a growing awareness amongst home anglers that the same fish which they pay dearly to angle for in fresh water are available free of charge (apart from the state licence) in the ocean. However, in order to capitalise on this, shoals of feeding sea trout must be located and careful note taken of their diurnal or seasonal movements. Sea trout kelts are often well-mended, handsome fish and it is only when they are being prepared for consumption that their rather anaemic white flesh is seen and their true status becomes apparent to the inexperienced angler. In some districts (eg Moy and Ballyshannon) there is good sea trout fishing in April and May. It is my belief that the majority of fish taken are kelts and consideration should be given to altering the closed season accordingly.

Sea trout may be caught in a wide range of different marine habitats, from the tangled, matted kelp beds of the Connemara coastline to the wild surf beaches of Donegal, and from the urbanised estuaries of the Rivers Liffey and Dodder in Dublin to small, sandy, rock-strewn coves in the south-west. It is only really by trial and error that the feeding areas of saltwater trout may be found and this adds both zest and excitement to the quest. In general, the more likely sea trout haunts include sheltered bays or headlands, often containing strong growths of kelp or bladder-wrack. The fish move along such areas on the flood tide, feeding on a whole range of organisms such as pollack, coalfish, elvers, sandeels, sparling, marine worms, crustaceans, and a host of other marine invertebrates. During the summer months sea trout are more likely to be found chasing either concentrations of sandeel or shoals of small sparling or whitebait. Sea trout are often found alongside bass and, when fishing new locations, known bass marks are a good starting point. As the tide ebbs, the fish often hover behind large obstacles in the tide, such as rocky outcrops, collapsed walls or even old breakwaters; in this way their food is conveyed to them on the tide. When the tide is ebbing hard the sea trout often concentrate almost exclusively on sandeel.

Prime times at sea

For daytime fishing, stealth and concealment are of the utmost importance and one should always fish at maximum distance. Do not forget that these are the same shy, retiring creatures which you stalk so delicately when fishing upriver. While sea trout will take during the day, it is at dusk, or into the early night, that they feed most consistently. When shore fishing you will find that spring tides invariably produce the best results.

As in night fishing on the river, the key to success is a good, low-water reconnaissance of the chosen area. I often find it useful to draw a small sketch-map of the area, simply to remind myself of its contours. Once flooded, a small bay or estuary becomes completely transformed and the sandbars, ridges and rocky outcrops are quickly forgotten.

You should also remember that it is feeding sea trout which you are seeking and not necessarily those massing to run the river. Very often, fish which are just about to enter a system have ceased to feed and as a consequence they behave more like salmon than sea trout. For this reason a small dinghy provides an ideal way to search a selection of small bays and inlets. It saves a great deal of travel time and gives you the freedom to try a range of locations at various stages of the tide. Sea trout are best fished from a drifting boat on the flood and from an anchored boat or from the shore as the tide ebbs.

Conventional wisdom in Ireland dictates that late May, June and July are the best months for sea trout fishing in salt water. However, winter fishing for sea trout has proven very successful in Scotland. Maiden sea trout are at sea throughout the winter period but how accessible they are to the Irish shore or inshore angler remains unknown. There is also some confusion regarding the legality of sea trout fishing during the closed freshwater season and one would be well advised to check with the local fisheries board before embarking on a midwinter expedition.

Spinning and bait fishing in the sea

Sea trout are taken by a range of methods in the sea. The majority of Irish sea-caught fish are taken on silver spinners, ranging from Tobys to plain, silver pike spoons. Devons (blue and silver), Mepps and small plugs are also used. Bait fishing is normally carried out with either sandeel or mackerel strip. The sandeels are mounted using a single size 4 hook which is passed through the upper and lower lips. I find that the addition of a small size 16 treble about two-thirds of the way along the body solves the problem of tail-nipping sea trout. A mackerel sliver is normally taken from the silver belly-skin and it may be fished either in conjunction with a spinner or on its own.

The tackle for spinning and bait fishing is a long (9ft; 2.5m) light rod and fixed-spool reel containing 8lb (3.5kg) nylon. The heavy nylon is necessary, for large sea trout may have to be 'horsed' out of bladder-wrack or kelp beds. A barrel lead is often necessary when long casts are required. However, if you approach your quarry with care you will find that they may move very close to the shore at times, particularly where a rockface falls off into 1 to 1.5m of water.

Fly fishing in the sea

Fly fishing in the sea is little practised in Ireland and the development of effective lures and techniques could provide an exciting challenge to the innovative angler. There is no reason why Falkus's standard sunk lure patterns should not work under Irish conditions. A whole new range of techniques and adaptations is surely waiting to be discovered. I have done a little sea fishing for sea trout with the fly and in my experience a slow-sinking sink-tip line is essential if one is to avoid the constant irritation of snagging seaweed. The tackle should be kept simple and relatively cheap, for no matter how careful you are, it will eventually become corroded by the salt water. Always thoroughly wash your items of equipment in fresh tap water on returning home from each trip to the sea.

Perhaps the most extraordinary feature of sea fishing for sea trout in Ireland is the seemingly disproportionate number of 3–5lb (1.5–2.5kg) fish which are taken. Falkus suggests that our coasts may play host to a range of feeding fish from Scotland, Wales and England, but I think this unlikely. My own view is that the sea angler takes a more representative share of the various sizes of sea trout present; for even the multi-spawners will feed ravenously at sea. The numbers of large fish are only disproportionate when contrasted with the freshwater catch, which is mainly composed of finnock and maidens.

CHAPTER 4

BROWN TROUT

Location

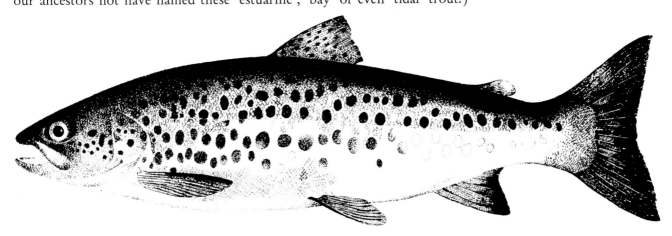

Life cycle and biology

Brown trout have been, and hopefully will continue to be, synonymous with all that is fresh, wild and traditional in the Irish countryside, for they are the commonest and most widely distributed of our freshwater fishes. Since the migratory ancestors of our present-day resident brown trout first forged upstream from the post-glacial seas some 10 000 years ago, they have permeated every freshwater catchment in the country. They are found in abundance in high, isolated lakes 500 to 800m above sea level; verification of their presence in these lakes often necessitates a three- or four-hour climb. They are equally abundant in the rich lowland rivers and lakes of the central plain and are found in shallow estuaries and bays where they are known by that most unappealing and inappropriate of names 'slob trout'. (Why could our ancestors not have named these 'estuarine', 'bay' or even 'tidal' trout?)

Variable characteristics

The brown trout is a highly adaptable fish and varies greatly in growth rate, coloration and even in its behaviour, depending on its physical and biological habitat.

The coloration of the various races of brown trout often reflects their dietary habits; some fish feed almost exclusively on creatures from one stratum of their watery world. Perhaps the best known example of this form of exclusivity is the gillaroo of the great western lakes. Their name is a derivative of the Irish *giolla rua* meaning the 'red fellow' or the 'red servant'. They are the

83

most beautifully marked creatures, with yellow or light golden brown fins, and their flanks are covered by vivid, bright orange-red spots. Their brown backs contrast markedly with the reddish-brown of the underbelly. Their strong, thick-walled, muscular stomachs or gizzards are developed for crushing snails and crustaceans picked from amongst the rocks. Sleek, black-finned, surface-feeding sonaghan and the deep, fish-feeding, ferox are also physically distinguishable by the angler.

Traditional taxonomists have always tended towards differentiating between the various races of brown trout on purely morphological characteristics and all were given a bright, fine-sounding Latin name. For example, the Scottish Lough Leven trout were titled *Salmo levenensis*, ferox were *Salmo ferox*, the sea trout were *Salmo trutta* and the common brown trout *Salmo fario*. However, in latter years the pragmatists came to the fore amongst taxonomists and in the interests of reducing piscatorial discrimination on the basis of race or colour, all trout, including sea trout, were declared to be one species, *Salmo trutta*. However, Andy Ferguson, from Queen's University Belfast, has

L. Arrow, Co. Sligo; one of Ireland's premier brown trout, dry-fly loughs

now shown that the brown trout of Lough Melvin are composed of at least three genetically distinct races of trout. Indeed he states: 'There are good grounds for treating gillaroos, sonaghan and ferox as distinct and separate species of trout.' These specific races maintain their integrity by spawning in distinctly different locations. The gillaroo spawn in the lake margins near the outflowing Drowse River or in the outflow itself, the sonaghan spawn the inflowing rivers and the ferox utilise one specific deep glide in one of the inflowing rivers.

However, the essential difference between the brown trout and the migratory salmonids which we have discussed so far is that the brown trout, both as a juvenile and as an adult, feeds and grows in fresh water, often within a well-defined geographical location. Some riverine trout show little tendency to migrate and may live their full life cycle within a few short kilometres of stream. In the larger midland and western lakes, trout may undertake long spawning migrations covering several months; some of these may commence as early as mid to late August and at times these migratory brown trout may be as difficult and dour as any stale salmon. At other times, however, particularly in mid to late September, they may become aggressive and more prone to feed. At such times they fall easy prey to the unscrupulous angler who may take from the river bags of twenty or more of these large 2lb+ (1kg+) lake trout with relative ease. Despite the fact that the flesh is of poor quality, this practice continues. As a conservation method, a statutory ban on fishing in prescribed rivers (eg Finny, Joyce's River, Owenriff River, etc) throughout September is long overdue.

Spawning

Time of spawning is also variable amongst various brown trout stocks but in general where salmon are present in a system in any great numbers, trout have a tendency to spawn from late October to mid-November. In the midlands, the bulk of the fish run the streams in early to mid-December. However, in these midland areas the trout spawn in groups and it is not unusual to have a prolonged spawning season with fish moving onto the redds from mid-October to mid-January.

The spawning act itself, the digging and covering of the eggs and the hatching process of ovum, eyed ovum, yolk-sac fry and alevin is analogous to both the sea trout and the salmon. The young trout have a tendency to take up residence in the pool areas of the stream and are highly aggressive in their territoriality. Since they are laid earlier than the salmon, they also hatch some three to four weeks before the salmon. This incremental size advantage is used to the full by the young trout who are most adept at ensuring that the salmon are confined to the faster water above the pool areas. In situations where trout are absent, salmon are quite happy to colonise pool areas normally regarded as trout-only zones.

Maturity in brown trout is also variable. In some systems the trout spawn annually after reaching sexual maturity, which is normally at three to four years of age. However, in the majority of Irish lake systems fish spawn every second year and thus some 50 per cent of the population is in prime condition throughout the year. Anglers often marvel at the condition of some trout which they catch in February or March. They mistakenly assume that the trout spawned early and took full advantage of the 'mild winter weather' to regain condition. The rigours of spawning take an appreciable toll amongst brown trout and the majority of a given year-class will have died off within two to three years of reaching maturity. Various stocks or strains of trout may reach maturity at varying rates, but in general trout adopt one of two strategies; they are either fast growing, early maturing fish or slower growing, late maturing fish. It is often these late maturing trout that give rise to the larger 'trophy' trout in a system.

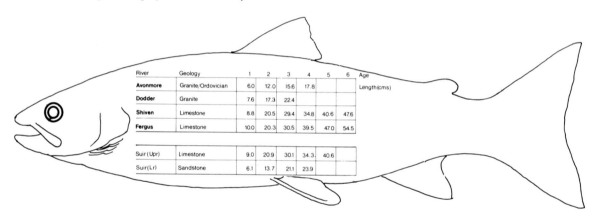

River	Geology	1	2	3	4	5	6	Age
Avonmore	Granite/Ordovician	6.0	12.0	15.6	17.8			Length (cms)
Dodder	Granite	7.6	17.3	22.4				
Shiven	Limestone	8.8	20.5	29.4	34.8	40.6	47.6	
Fergus	Limestone	10.0	20.3	30.5	39.5	47.0	54.5	
Suir (Upr)	Limestone	9.0	20.9	30.1	34.3	40.6		
Suir (Lr)	Sandstone	6.1	13.7	21.1	23.9			

Growth rates

Brown trout growth rates vary enormously from system to system. To illustrate this point I have included growth charts for brown trout from the Dodder River, County Dublin, the Avonmore River, County Wicklow, the River Shiven, County Galway, the River Suir, County Tipperary, and the River Fergus, County Clare. In these illustrations the improving growth rates may be directly related to the presence of an increasing proportion of softer sandstones and limestones in the catchments. I have also included a growth chart for trout from the upper and lower Suir. As may be seen from the diagram, the growth rate of trout in the upper Suir is equivalent to that of the Fergus, but that of the lower Suir is intermediate between the Dodder and the Shiven growth rates. The reason may be the influence of softer waters flowing from the lower Suir tributaries such as the Clodiagh, Tar and Blackwater, which neutralise the richer limestone water flowing from the upper catchment. Increased juvenile densities, in the main channel, due to increased recruitment from the gravel-laden streams, may also be a major contributory factor.

Lifespan

Brown trout are not long-lived fish and six to seven years is their normal maximum lifespan. However, some late maturing fish may live well into their teens. Recent comparative biological work has shown that scale analysis, which up to now has been considered *the* definitive method of ageing fish, may not be as accurate as previously thought. Analysis of earstones or otoliths and scales from long-lived trout have shown that once a fish has ceased to grow, its calcareous coat of scales has no need to expand further and thus no further annuli or winter bands appear on the scales. The animal, however, continues to lay down clear age bands on its earstones. Fish which would have been aged at eight plus, by scale reading have been shown by otolith analysis to be nearer fifteen! Thankfully, from the biologist's point of view, such long-lived fish are a rarity and only occur in situations where poor growth rate is combined with a low stock density.

Lake stocks

Stock surveys of Loughs Conn and Melvin, in 1986 and 1987, have indicated populations of approximately 500 000 and 300 000 brown trout, over 8in (20cm) long, respectively. Lough Sheelin in the mid-seventies had a population of 100 000 trout for its 4000 acres (1600ha). These fish are not evenly spread throughout the fishery but are concentrated in the productive areas of the lake. Thus densities of 50/100 trout per productive acre are not uncommon in Irish lakes. Even heavy stockings of fish-farm trout will add little more than five or six trout per productive acre of the smaller midland lakes.

Anglers are notoriously inefficient at harvesting respectable percentages of the available crop. Even on the midland lakes, such as Lough Owel, where angling pressure is consistently high and a greater percentage of stocked two-year-old trout is available to the angler, exploitation rates generally vary between 5 and 10 per cent. In the large western lakes rates may drop as low as 1 or 2 per cent. The majority of mature Irish lake brown trout die of old age.

Confusion has arisen regarding the strains of brown trout used in stocking Irish waters and their ultimate effect on the genetics of the wild stocks. Even in Lough Sheelin where over the years millions of Roscrea strain fish-farm trout were stocked as ova, fry, yearlings, two-year-olds, or even brood stock, a genetic profile of the wild adults has shown less than an 8 per cent genetic influence.

The main reason for this is that fish-farm trout contribute little to the spawning stocks of any system into which they are introduced. When stocked as fry they are generally outcompeted by the more wily wild fry and few reach maturity. When stocked as yearlings or two-year-olds directly into the lake, the fish are constantly harassed by resident wild fish and are forced into the less productive areas. They are also driven away from stream mouths at spawning time. These stocked trout (one-year-olds and two-year-olds) have not been imprinted on any specific stream in the catchment and so they lack the strong, specific reproductive force which drives wild fish up their native streams. There is also some circumstantial evidence that even where they manage to run a stream, they are severely harassed on the redds by the wild trout.

Lake stocking is generally carried out in waters where natural recruitment is less than the parent water may accommodate. This may be due to the small size of the native streams (Lough Owel) or to pollution and/or drainage (Lough Sheelin, Lough Mask). In such situations the fish farm stockie is an ideal management alternative. It grows well, can remain in the fishery for a further two or three seasons, and has little, if any, effect on the wild strain of fish. The art of stocking one- or two-year-old trout is plugging known gaps in the natural recruitment cycle. Thanks to the pioneering work of Martin O'Grady of the Central Fisheries Board, such stock assessment in our midland lakes is now part and parcel of the ongoing management programme.

Typical length frequency distribution for parr and adult brown trout from a limestone river

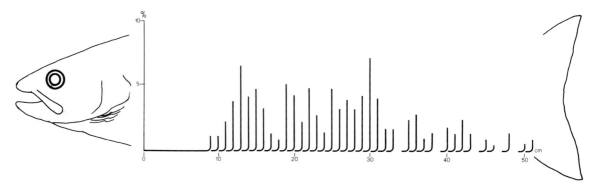

River stocks

Because of their confined nature, stock levels in riverine fisheries, particularly those of takable size, are far less dramatic than those listed above. However, in areas less than 2m deep the whole stream is productive and appreciable densities may be recorded. In one 3km section of the Upper Bunowen River near Ahascragh, County Galway, I consistently obtained, over a four-year period, population estimates of 2500 to 3000 brown trout, between 4 and 10in (10–25cm) in length. This is exceptional, for even in the most productive of waters the usual estimates are 500 to 600 trout for a 3km section.

Anglers tend to overestimate the numbers of larger fish available to them in a season. Generally there are no more than ten trout over 2lb (1kg) and three over 4lb (2kg) present in each 3km section of even the most productive streams. In over fifteen years of electrically fishing some of the most productive waters in Ireland, I have come across no more than six trout over 6lb (2.5kg). However, electrical currents are quickly dissipated in depths greater than 2m and there may have been more larger fish lurking in the depths.

Stocking trout into rivers has less long-term effects than stocking them into lakes, for even with moderate angling pressure, over 80 per cent of the stocked fish are normally taken by anglers in a period of ten to twelve weeks.

In both river and lake systems, one of the main advantages of stocking some takable brown trout is that it results in a greater harvest of wild trout. It is well documented that freshly stocked trout are very catholic (some would say stupid) in their taste and in conjunction with natural food organisms their stomachs will often contain stones, pebbles, feathers, reed stems, small twigs, etc. While adapting to natural food, they are easy prey for the angler and as a result catch rates increase. This encourages anglers to fish longer and more intensively, even when the bulk of the stocked fish have either adapted to natural food and are harder to catch or have been taken from the fishery. As a consequence of this increased fishing effort, the catch of wild fish also increases.

Exploitation
Angling exploitation rates on river systems may be appreciably higher than those on lakes. This is particularly true in the case of the larger fish in the system. Because of the shape of the ecological pyramid the numbers of trout over 1lb (0.5kg) are limited. Anglers tend to concentrate their efforts on certain prime areas and careful management is required if these are to maintain stocks of quality trout. I would like to see the introduction of a national daily bag limit of four river trout and an overall possession limit of ten frozen or otherwise preserved trout.

Arterial drainage
Arterial drainage has a catastrophic effect on riverine systems. Stephen Swales, in a scientific paper which he published in 1981, has succinctly summarised the effects of such drainage on the physical equilibrium of rivers:

Streams and rivers are dredged and widened to reduce water levels and so increase the freeboard between the surface of the water and the outfalls of field underdrainage systems.

Such severe changes to morphology and hydrology of a river invariably eliminate many of its natural characteristics. Straightening a river, for example, reduces or removes its normal meandering pattern while deepening and widening work usually destroys the pool riffle pattern which is usually present in many parts of a river system. Dredging a river bed can also seriously affect its structure, composition and stability; stable gravel beds may be replaced by shifting bars of sand or silt, which are much more uniform. Bankside vegetation is also cleared to reduce the risk of trees falling into the river and obstructing flow, and to provide access to the river for excavating machinery.

River flow is one of the most important physical characteristics of a river to be affected by drainage works. The overall effect of drainage work is usually to increase the extremes of flow conditions, ie increased flow during times of high discharge and reduced flow during times of low discharge. Since most aquatic organisms are adapted to only a relatively narrow range of flow conditions, an increase to the extremes of the normal range may eliminate the less tolerant species. Also, water depth is reduced under normal flow conditions since the cross-sectional area of the river channel is usually increased by channel alterations, decreasing still further the 'living space available to plant and animal communities'.

Ironically, where the dredgers fail to reach below the gravel layers or in situations where they expose suitable gravel banks, the numbers of trout present after drainage may actually increase. However, these are predominantly one- and two-year-old trout, with few older fish. The average size is thus drastically lowered and is certainly far from enticing to the angler. Drainage removes all the deeper pool areas, the habitat of the larger trout. It also exposes large quantities of fresh gravel, ideal spawning ground for the trout. The unstable bottom holds large numbers of the more active mayfly nymphs, chironomid larvae, the black fly or *Simulium* larvae, but few crustaceans

Length frequency distribution for parr and adult brown trout from a drained limestone river. Note the absence of trout greater than 30cm

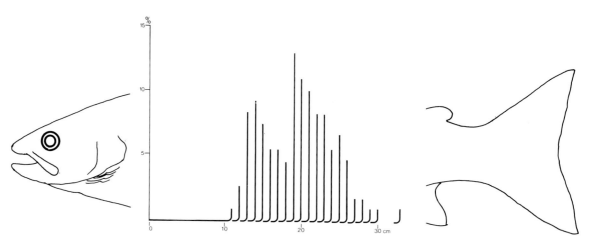

or snails are present. All these organisms are ideal food for the younger trout, and the population explodes. But the food source is limited, as is the availability of territories for the larger fish, so the trout becomes stunted and few survive after their first spawning. However, where the dredgers do reach below the gravel layers, a bed of organic silt is normally exposed. Since the bankside bushes and trees have been removed, all shade is gone and the rich organic mud is constantly irradiated by sunlight. Plants sprout luxuriantly in the new habitat. But these are not the original *soft* water weeds; they are great, hard bullrushes which impede the flow and reduce the effectiveness of the drainage scheme. They are also the cause of much of the maintenance cost of drainage.

The silty, soft bottom is completely unsuited to trout and is inhabited by minnow, stoneloach, sticklebacks and gudgeon. It provides an ideal habitat for resting pike and these can be found here waiting to make a sortie into the neighbouring trout zones.

It is heartening that in the recent past there has been a great change in attitude on the part of the drainage authorities and they are now making great efforts to rehabilitate previously drained systems. This change has undoubtedly been brought about by the more enlightened and sensitive approach of present-day engineers and by European influences, which insist that drainage schemes should be environmentally acceptable before EC funding is forthcoming. Unfortunately, large amounts of money and effort are now having to be expended on rehabilitation programmes, which would not have been necessary were it not for the intransigence of past design engineers. They saw the rivers as inanimate physical channels whose principal function was to flush fresh water towards the sea at the fastest possible rate. Where nature had failed to ensure maximum discharge over the shortest possible time period, the drainage engineers stepped in to 'improve' the situation — regardless of the ecological consequences. Various fisheries administrations must also share the blame for allowing this catastrophe to happen and settling for quite inadequate re-stocking programmes. A firm, constructive stand by those in authority could have brought about a compromise scheme where long-term damage to fisheries could have been minimised.

Fortunately, many drained limestone catchments are beginning to show signs of recovery. Economic recession has resulted in a reduced level of maintenance and rivers have benefited. The rehabilitation programmes are also having their effect and overall the situation is improving. However, the visiting angler will find the banks of many of these drained rivers artificially high and difficult and at times dangerous to fish.

Fly fishing

Irish brown trout are taken by all legitimate methods throughout the angling season. However, the majority of trout are taken on the artificial fly, and since it is also the most rewarding and enjoyable method to use, I intend to concentrate initially on fly fishing for brown trout in both lake and river. As in the case of the migratory salmonids, I have included a section on alternative methods at the end of the chapter.

To become an efficient fly angler it is necessary to know not alone the basic biology and behaviour patterns of the primary quarry (the trout), but also of the quarry's quarry (its food). A sound knowledge of the periods of emergence of the more important insects and a knowledge of the behaviour and life cycles of the common snails, crustaceans and smaller fodder fish will ensure consistent success. Under each sub-section I have therefore included a brief description of the more important food items and their period of importance in the trout's diet.

Fly fishing in lakes

There are a great many different types of trout lake in Ireland but for the sake of clarity I have attempted to classify them into the following four categories: large limestone lakes, smaller limestone lakes, neutrally and moderately acid lakes, and acid lakes.

Large limestone lakes
These big sheets of water (2000–40 000 acres; 800–16 000ha) present conditions more or less peculiar to Ireland. Characteristically, they are fairly shallow, with a bed of stones and sand and areas of mud and/or silt. They hold coarse fish as well as trout, are situated on the limestone plains, are rich in food, and produce red-fleshed trout of excellent quality and good size.

There are two sub-types. The first, of which Lough Derravaragh and Lough Arrow are examples, lies entirely on the limestone and has a very high pH value, 8.4 or over. The water, outside of peak plankton periods, is extremely transparent, as the lime has the effect of precipitating all suspended matter. Lakes of this sub-type produce very fast-growing, thick-set, silvery trout, the average size of which may be 1½lb (680g) or over. Trout of 3–4lb (1.5–2kg) will likely feature in any catch of half a dozen fish. Ferox trout are not very common in this kind of highly alkaline lake.

The second category of big limestone lake, of which Lough Corrib and Lough Mask are examples, has a somewhat lower pH value, and less transparent water. The trout of such lakes tend to be more bronze in colour, and the average size is usually less, somewhere between 1 and 1¼lb (450–570g). However, these lakes yield more trout of 10lb (4.5kg) and over than do the highly alkaline lakes. These big trout, running up to 20lb (9kg) or more, and usually in very good condition, are not very old fish. The age range is, as a rule, eight years to twelve years.

Early-hatching flies
At the beginning of the season, in March and early April, the limestone-lake trout feed extensively on shrimps or snails. While small chironomids hatch off and on during the spring, amongst the first sizeable flies to emerge in quantity on the limestone lakes is the lake olive (*Cloeon simile*) which hatches under mild conditions in April and May.

In the highly alkaline lakes, a large, dark chironomid, the duckfly (*Chironomus anthracinus*), hatches in the latter part of March and early April and usually produces a good rise of fish. Sometimes the winged fly is taken, and a dry fly kills. At other times, the pupa is taken, often just below the surface film when it is about to hatch.

The mayfly (*Ephemera danica*) hatches on the limestone lakes about the middle of May. It continues to hatch for about three weeks, though stragglers may appear for weeks afterwards.

The time of the hatch on any given water varies somewhat from year to year according to weather conditions. The rate of development of the nymphs is affected by the weather in early spring, which can advance or retard their readiness to develop into winged insects in May by as much as a week either way.

The nymphs swim up from the bottom to the surface and change into so-called greendrakes. In soft weather, that is when there is a fair degree of humidity, they ride on the surface for a period while their wings are expanding and drying. Then — if a trout hasn't taken them! — they fly to the bushes on the shore. They have a special preference for hawthorn and alder bushes.

Trout feed on the ascending nymphs. If very large hatches are taking place, and huge numbers of nymphs are swimming up, or if the greendrakes are flying off the water very quickly, the trout may more or less ignore the greendrakes and feed chiefly on the nymphs.

In the bushes the greendrakes undergo a further moult into the spinner or imago stage. The imago is the final, mature stage. In the evening, the males (blackdrakes), which are smaller and darker than the females, dance in clouds over the bushes. The females, or greendrakes, fly from the bushes where they are sheltering when they are ready to mate. Mating takes place in the air, and the females may either return to the shelter of the bushes for a short while or fly out over the water, dipping several times on the surface to shed their eggs. When the eggs are all deposited, the females may continue to fly for a little while, but then they fall on the surface, where they flutter for a time before dying with wings outspread. These are the 'spent flies' or 'spent gnat'. The males also fall on the water.

Other food items
As the mayfly comes to an end, shoals of tiny perch fry, hatched from eggs deposited in late April, engage the attention of the trout — often for a time, to the exclusion of every other kind of food.

The great red sedge or murrough (*Phryganea grandis*) is sometimes plentiful in late May and June, and alders also occur on the water. Mid-June to late July is usually a slack period for trout fishing on the big limestone lakes.

Towards the end of July, the perch fry have become bigger and faster, and the shoals have been reduced and scattered by predation. Trout are therefore more inclined to take an interest in other foods. Large numbers of daddy-long-legs usually find their way, at intervals, on to the water, and the trout often rise well to them. The natural daddy (or 'harry' as it is often called) is extensively used for dapping.

From late July onwards, on calm, mild evenings, there are usually large numbers of sedges on the water. There is often a mixture of small and medium-sized species of silverhorns and brown, red and cinnamon sedges. Especially in the more alkaline lakes the trout often rise well to the sedges, and the dry-fly fishing may be quite good. In many waters, various species of *Phryganea*, such as the big grey-brown murrough (*P. striata*) and the smaller green peter and dark peter may hatch at dusk. Some of these, on certain waters, are very large flies. They emerge in open water, and swim rather than fly to the shore, making a strong ripple.

Smaller limestone lakes

These lakes, of anything from 20–500 acres (50–1200ha), can be subdivided, like the larger lakes, into the highly alkaline (pH 8.2 or more), with crystal-clear water, very rich fauna, and big silvery trout, and the less alkaline (pH 7.6 or below), with less clear water, and trout averaging 12–16oz (340–450g), though growing much larger. Fishing throughout the season follows the same general pattern as in the larger lakes.

Neutral and moderately acid lakes

These lakes are mostly of small or moderate size, but occasionally may be fairly big sheets of water (eg the Killarney lakes). They are located on and/or drain mainly granite or sandstone regions, and are, on the whole, at higher elevations than the limestone lakes. The pH varies from about 6.5 to 7.0 according to the amount of limestone occurring, whether as bedrock or as glacial drift. The water is moderately transparent; vegetation is adequate but rarely lush; and the fauna, while varied and fairly abundant, is never as rich as in high pH waters. The average size of trout varies from about three to the pound to about half a pound (150–220g), depending on conditions. In some lakes, trout of 1lb (0.5kg) and upwards are not infrequently taken on the fly. In the larger lakes, ferox-type trout running to 10lb (4.5kg) and over may occur.

Flies and other insects

The mayfly is usually absent, though it occurs in a few lakes of this type. Most important flies are chironomids and claret duns (*Leptophlebia* spp.), in addition to or instead of lake olives; sedges (mostly small and medium-sized forms), and land insects including ants, moths and beetles. Such lakes usually provide good wet-fly fishing, especially in March, April, May and September, as well as dry-fly fishing on summer evenings.

Acid lakes

These are lakes of small or moderate size, mostly in hilly or mountainous regions of acid rock. They may be partly or largely surrounded by bog, or may drain bog. The water may be comparatively clear (because of the scarcity of plankton rather than precipitation of suspended solids), or may be very brown owing to the presence of peat-bog drainage. The pH varies from 4.5 to 6.5. The trout are bronze or dark coloured and nearly always white fleshed. In general, acid lakes carry a big stock of small trout (3–4oz; 80–120g) and in many such lakes a half-pound trout is a big one. The fish are mainly caught on wet flies which are taken freely throughout the season.

Boat fishing

Throughout the season trout will be found feeding in open water on zooplankton or on macroinvertebrates and small fish in the littoral or productive areas of the lake. The extent of this latter zone is a highly variable factor and is dependent on the clarity of the water (which regulates light penetration), the lake contours and the substratum type. In really clear limestone lakes, such as Lough Owel, weed growth penetrates to depths of 10m or more, but this is the exception and in general the productive zone does not extend much beyond 5 or 6m. In the bigger lakes it is important to tap a good source of local knowledge before venturing out on these larger sheets of water; information on which areas are fishing well or where hatches of insects are likely to occur can make all the difference between success and failure.

Trout behaviour

Because of the density of invertebrate fauna in the limestone lakes, the trout are considered dour by the fly angler. The reason is simple, the trout's bottom larder is so well stocked that only an exceptional hatch of insects will entice it to feed mid-water or near the surface. In contrast, the neutral or moderately acid lakes, such as the lower lake in Killarney, normally provide more lively fishing. The trout are, of necessity, more opportunistic in their behaviour patterns and are much more inclined to alternate between bottom, mid-water and surface feeding. It is not unusual to catch trout in these lakes on dry fly or pupae which are stuffed with a fresh feed of snails or shrimp.

Daytime boat fishing

Daytime boat fishing is normally most productive between early April and mid-June and again in September. Peak fishing times are generally between 10.00 am and 1.30 pm and between 2.30 pm and 4.00 pm. However, if duckfly are about, be prepared for a late evening rise — even in late March and on the coldest of evenings!

The traditional Irish pattern of lake fishing is to let the boat off, at the full, unimpeded mercy of the wind, on a long drift over a kilometre or more of continuous shallows. A team of three wet flies are normally fished, on a floating line, near the surface. Short, snappy casts are the order of the day and it is surprising just how effective this technique may prove at times. However, with improving gear technology and a growing awareness of trout behaviour, the more innovative anglers are beginning to experiment with British reservoir techniques, such as sink-tip or sinking lines, lures, echo-sounders, drogues, leeboards, rudders, and with considerable success. The use of such deepwater methods has resulted in more consistent success, particularly with the early season trout feeding on fish, snail or shrimp.

The importance of good boatmanship

When lough fishing for sea trout, consistent success is as much about good boatmanship (see page 72 for information on new boat technology) as it is about good angling. This is also true in the case of brown trout, except that we must add the additional ingredient of a working knowledge of the feeding behaviour of the fish. The novice angler will soon learn that on drifting an area of lake several times in a row, he will come across a patch where fish are risen on each drift. It never ceases to amaze me how often anglers will continue to take a full drift on such occasions rather than rationalising what is happening and then taking appropriate action. In general, the boat is passing through an area of invertebrate activity where the trout are concentrated — the proverbial hotspot. The angler should either take shorter drifts near the area of activity, without using the engine, or he should anchor just off the taking zone and fish towards the feeding fish. When a trout is caught, a quick autopsy — a long-bladed filleting knife is very handy on these occasions — should reveal the reason for the feverish activity. At times, such a zone may extend across rather than downwind, following a definite contour line, and a leeboard can ensure a drift in the necessary direction.

When a strong wind is blowing, the breaking waves may whip up a great deal of white froth and foam. This becomes concentrated into wind lanes which are seen as long, relatively calm white streaks amongst the tossing waves. Emerging insects, or terrestrial insects which have been blown onto the water, may become trapped in these lanes and as a consequence they should be fished very carefully. If the froth is heavy, it has the effect of making even wet flies float on the surface. The best area to fish is just below the surface, under the foam, and therefore both flies and casts should be dipped in some sinking solution.

The large western lakes such as Mask, Corrib and Conn are really shallow, windswept, inland seas and the assistance of a competent gillie is not just useful but essential both to safety and angling success. The midland lakes are less dangerous but should not be taken for granted. Each lake has one particular wind which blows either straight down, or down and slightly across, the long axis of the lake. Such winds can instil tremendous power into waves even though the fetch may be no more than 5–10km. Be particularly careful of such winds and, again, seek local information on the advisability of fishing under such conditions.

A three-pounder, on the dry sedge, from L. Ennell, Co. Westmeath

Evening boat fishing

Evening boat fishing is generally concentrated into the midsummer period of mid-June to mid-August, but as mentioned previously, strong evening rises may occur at any time throughout the season. Evening fishing is almost exclusively concerned with deceiving surface or sub-surface feeding fish, which are generally taking either buzzers (chironomids), mayflies or sedges.

An evening rise may be encountered at any time from 6.00 pm to 1.00 or 2.00 am, depending on the insects which are about. However, the major feeding activity occurs immediately before or just following dusk. The wind often dies at this time and apart from a gentle swell or ripple, the surface of the lake is normally quite calm and the rate of drift is civilised. There is generally no need for drogues or anchors but a leeboard can prove useful at times.

Buzzers and sedges are taken as either emerging pupae, adults or ovipositing adults. Mayflies (which include both the olives and the true mayfly) are taken either as egg-laying spinners or in the case of *E. danica* as evening-hatching nymphs. The great attraction of evening fishing is the fact that the larger, predominantly bottom-feeding trout may be tempted to the surface. Balling buzzers (concentrations of ovipositing chironomids), a strong fall of spent gnat or a hatch of great murroughs or green peters constitute a really worthwhile feast for even the most fastidious snail or fish feeder.

Special considerations

As the wind drops, the angler should confine the use of his engine to the centre of the lake and row himself both into and out of potential feeding areas. Have regard for your fellow anglers and their choice of fishing area. When it is dark, always assume that you are surrounded by hidden boats which are continuing to fish, for there is nothing more annoying than the sudden great roar and splutter of a 10 or 12 hp engine across the lake's flat, calm surface where you are expecting trout to rise at any moment.

Light and shadow are also of vital concern to the evening angler and he should be ever vigilant that the shadows which he and his boat are casting are not acting as a deterrent to the trout. When the surface of the lake is hit by a low, bright sun, try donning polaroids and fishing into the sun. You will be surprised at how your success rate improves.

Shore fishing

Shore angling for brown trout is little practised in Ireland except in the smaller limestone or sandstone lakes. This is a great pity, for shore angling is immensely satisfying and at times highly effective — even in the larger lakes. It may be carried out either from the main shoreline itself or from the shore of suitable islands. The points of islands, particularly where they quickly shelve off to 2 or 3m of water are ideal locations for the shore angler.

The shore angler is normally fishing for either surface-feeding fish taking pupae, nymphs or adult insects or is seeking bottom-feeding fish which are concentrated into the stony, marginal areas near the shore. Surface feeders are easily spotted and may require long casts and wading. Shore-feeding fish may be in half a metre of water or less, right up against the stones, so all of the near water should be carefully fished before wading out into the lake margins. At times, these bottom-feeding fish may be identified by a series of tiny rings made by their moving tails breaking the surface as they grub about vertically amongst the stones.

I remember one noteworthy occasion when I encountered fish feeding on snails at the edge of one of the islands in Kilnahard Bay on Lough Sheelin. Tails were breaking the surface all along the perimeter of the island and it took me several minutes to convince myself that it was actually feeding fish which were making the disturbance. Using a three-fly cast of two Black and Peacock Spiders and a leaded nymph on the point, I managed to take five trout, averaging 1½lb (680g), in just three casts! I was fishing from a boat which kept drifting away from the feeding area. Had I beached the boat and fished the shoreline, I am sure my bag would have been even heavier.

Wading

It is often tempting to wade in order to gain that elusive extra metre or two. However, remember that lake trout, unlike their river brethren, are unlikely to stop feeding when they sense a disturbance in the water; they simply move out a further ten or twenty metres from the shore. When deep wading, unless you are exceptionally circumspect in your movements, you will simply drive the line of feeding trout out further. To avoid this problem I adopt my 10m/five minute routine. I wade out 10 to 15m, wait for five minutes or so and again wade out a further 10m. Generally you will need to wade no further than 30 to 40m. When you have perfected the required stealth you will find fish rising on both sides of you, and as evening approaches you may fish towards the shore if required. This is particularly useful when the sinking sun backs onto the shore.

Irish lake margins, particularly the limestone lakes, can be exceptionally dangerous. They are often coated in a layer of thick, glutinous marl which initially gives the impression of firmness but quite quickly takes hold of a boot as the angler's weight forces it further and further into the marl. With nothing to give you purchase, you will find it impossible to extricate yourself. If you are trapped in such a situation, face towards the shore and lie forward into the water. Your waders will either pull free from the marl or your feet and legs may be pulled clear of the waders. Once free, do not hesitate or attempt to stand upright but scramble, lizard-

like, towards the shore. By spreading your body-weight and making use of your buoyancy in the water, the marl will support you until you reach the shore.

Casting

In the smaller lakes, where wading is dangerous, long casting is often necessary to cover feeding fish adequately and consistently. It is also a great advantage when lure fishing, since it gives the angler an opportunity to vary his retrieve and alter the speed and depth of the bait. Some anglers may become obsessed with distance to the exclusion of all else. I remember in the sixties when Pallas Lake near Tullamore, County Offaly, was Mecca for many Dubliners, a race of anglers nicknamed the p-pot fishermen appeared. These men were dedicated 'brood-stockers' and their main enjoyment lay in developing new lines, new rods and techniques which would increase their distance. I was intrigued by these individuals as they stood at the end of the long, wooden fishing stands, babies' baths strapped low around their loins (these were used as line trays), and using a stiff-armed, unorthodox, double-haul technique, they could shoot out 35 or 40m of line with relative ease. They were my heroes for many years, until it began to dawn on me that they were not terribly good at catching fish. Granted, they consistently caught their limit of freshly stocked broodies in the early season, but so did many other, less capable, casters. When fishing for feeding fish later in the season they should have shown a clear advantage, but they did not. Their preoccupation with distance had left little time for developments at the business end of the equipment — the fly.

Early season

When fishing for non-rising fish the shore angler is well advised to keep moving and to consistently alternate his techniques until he locates where and on what the fish are feeding. He may also start fishing earlier than his boat-fishing colleague, for shore angling in March can be most productive. I invariably start the season using a fast-sinking line and a size 8 Baby Doll or Black Chenille lure. Spring seems to be a time of simplicity, but extremes. In spring I have no idea why trout should prefer black rather than white on alternate days, under similar conditions, but I can guarantee you that they often do.

Dry fly

Summer shore fishing provides an opportunity to fish the dry fly. When fish are feeding heavily on dry buzzers, sedges or olives, they invariably follow a set beat or path through the hatching zone. The shore angler may capitalise on this behaviour by placing himself in an appropriate position and casting to feeding fish. If he fishes carefully he may cause little disturbance, even when landing

100

fish, and the feeding frenzy may proceed about him while he extracts six or more trout from his chosen location. Exact imitations are hard to beat when fishing for surface-feeding fish and the angler would be well advised to buy some local patterns of the more common insects. Even if he ties his own flies, he may find his imitations of a particular insect a shade too bright or too dark to suit local conditions. A purchased tying is never wasted for it may be copied for future use.

Dapping

This is a very popular method of catching brown trout and the principle is exactly that described previously for sea trout (see page 88). In the case of brown trout, however, both the natural mayfly and the larger sedges (peters and murroughs) are also used as bait. Some anglers prefer a dapping cocktail, and it is not unusual to see a daddy/grasshopper combination in use. On some lakes, such as Lough Corrib, the dap is consistently far more effective than the artificial dry fly during the peak of the mayfly hatch.

LAKE FISHING FOR BROWN TROUT

EQUIPMENT

Rods

For general boat fishing a 10–11ft (3–3.5m) carbon fibre rod is ideal. For dry-fly fishing a stiff action 8½–9ft (2.5m) rod is required. Many lake anglers carry two ready-mounted rods — a wet-fly and a dry-fly rod. The visiting angler will find a general-purpose 9ft (2.5m) rod quite adequate for both types of fishing. For shore fishing a good quality 9–10ft (2.5–3m) stiff-action reservoir rod is ideal. It may be used for all types of shore fishing, from lure to dry fly. Other aspects of tackle for lake trout (reels, lines, leaders, etc) were dealt with in the context of the sea trout (see page 75) and apply equally to fishing for both brown and rainbow trout.

Fly fishing in rivers

Rivers and streams may vary considerably in character throughout their course as the gradient changes. They may pass from one type of geological formation to another or receive large tributaries which flow over radically different rock strata. However, it is possible to define seven typical 'river' types. In some instances, one large river may display several of these zones throughout its course. For example, the River Liffey rises in the Wicklow hills as a typical acid stream, which receives a run of lake trout from Blessington Lake; below Ballymore Eustace it develops all the characteristics of a typical moorland stream; below Kildare it moves onto a bed of carboniferous limestone and radically changes character in a few short kilometres to a typical wet- and dry-fly river. By the time it reaches Straffan, County Kildare, it has become a fully fledged limestone trout stream; indeed, some of the fastest growing Irish brown trout ever recorded came from the Liffey at Lucan — just outside Dublin city. It is obvious then that any classification which we make must be arbitrary.

Limestone rivers and streams of high pH value

For all practical purposes, there are no chalk streams in Ireland. Some of the limestone rivers and streams, however, are very similar in general character to the chalk streams of the south of England. These rivers and streams provide mainly dry-fly fishing and nymph fishing; but in the more streamy sections there is wet-fly fishing in spring.

Waters in this category vary in size, from rivers 30m or more in width to insignificant brooks less than 3m wide, but sometimes 1m deep. These lesser brooks may produce surprisingly good trout, up to 3lb (1.5g) in weight and in excellent condition, and should not be discounted. Broadly speaking, the average weight of trout in high pH rivers and streams is between ¾lb and 1lb (340–450g), with 3 and 4lb (1.5–2kg) fish a possibility.

Because limestone waters are fed to a large extent by surface drainage, they fluctuate in level throughout the season more than do chalk streams. May, June and September provide, in general, the best fishing, but, given reasonable water, there may be good, if difficult, evening fishing in July and August.

These limestone waters, particularly where rather swift stony reaches alternate with glides and pools, may produce an immense variety of insects. Fortunately for the angler, however, trout are not entomologists, and there are only a few species of fly which the fish seem to single out to the exclusion of all others. Outside of periods when such flies are hatching in quantity, generalised patterns which suggest the type of fly most abundant at the time will usually kill fish.

The most important natural flies on rivers and streams of the category under consideration are the following:

1. Large dark olive (*Baetis rhodani*) — Mainly March and April.

2. Various olives and pale wateries (species of *Baetis* and *Centroptilum*) — May to end of season.

3. Iron blue dun (*Baetis pumilus*) — Mainly April and May. On cold, showery days, trout often take it in preference to other flies on the water at the same time.

4. Pale evening dun (*Procloen rufulum*) — Mostly in slow-flowing rivers. May onwards. Late evening. When it hatches in quantity, trout may concentrate on it.

5. Blue-winged olive (*Ephemerella ignita*) — Summer, June onwards, but especially in July and August. Midday onwards, but mainly in the evening in hot weather. Singled out by trout, which sometimes concentrate on a particular stage of the fly, ie nymph, dun or spinner (sherry spinner).

6. Yellow evening dun (*Ephemerella notata*) — Localised. Mid-May to mid-June. Mainly in the evening. Nymphs come off weeds in fast shallows. Sometimes produces frantic, selective rise. Fish may concentrate on nymph, dun or spinner.

7. Fisherman's curse or grey midge (*Caenis* spp.) — Small, greyish flies. Some hatch in mornings, some in evenings. Summer. Usually in large numbers. Moult into spinners very soon after leaving water.

8. Mayfly — Late May and early June. River trout take all three stages: nymph, greendrake (dun), and spent (spinner).

9. Sedge — Especially in Munster, the caperer, *Sericostoma personatum*, hatches by day, in mayfly time, on limestone streams. This is a fair-sized, very dark coloured sedge. Trout often take it in preference to mayfly. On many rivers the grey flag sedges (*Hydropsyche* spp.) hatch by day during May, and bring on strong rises of trout. From June onwards various medium-sized and small sedges are on the water mainly in the evening, and produce good, business-like rises.

10. Hawthorn fly (*Bibio markii*) — A fair-sized dark dipteran (housefly group), which flies with a long pair of legs trailing, and is most abundant in the vicinity of hawthorn bushes. Chiefly in May. A land fly, but often gets on the water.

11. Black gnat (*Bibio johannis*) — Another land fly. Summer.

12. Reed smut (*Simulium* spp.) — Also referred to as black gnat. Larvae are aquatic, especially common in beds of buttercup in fast water. Adult is a small, hunched-shouldered black dipteran. Knotted midge is the best artificial pattern.

Wet-fly and dry-fly rivers

These are generally fair-sized rivers in which riffles regularly alternate with glides and pools. They are neutral to moderately alkaline and are suitable for all types of fishing. These rivers tend to run low in prolonged dry spells. Natural flies, much as in the previous category, are to be found, but fly life generally is not so abundant, though it may be very varied. Trout usually average about 6oz (170g), with 1lb (450g) fish plentiful, and good chance of bigger, especially with the dry fly.

Moorland rivers

These differ from the previous category mainly in that as a general rule the flow is swifter, riffles are more numerous than glides or pools, and the pH is usually lower. Wet fly is normally the best, and often fishing is most rewarding when there is a fair amount of water.

Acid, rocky streams

These usually hold plenty of trout, but the average size may be only 3oz (85g) and a ½lb (230g) fish would be a specimen.

Big, deep rivers

Often these are essentially coarse fish and/or salmon waters. The sluggish reaches may hold some big trout, and there is a good chance of taking an occasional heavy fish on a dry sedge or mayfly in the evening. The average size may be high, and fish of 3lb (1.5kg) or over may be encountered.

'Croneen' or 'Dollaghan' waters

'Croneen' is a midlands term for big lake trout that ascend tributary rivers and streams from about July onwards, and 'Dollaghan' are the equivalent trout from Lough Neagh. These trout, which can average as much as 2lb (1kg) in some cases, and grow to over 6lb (2.5kg), may travel a long way for a considerable time before spawning, and the habits of the fish are rather similar to those of sea trout or salmon.

Tidal waters

In the upper tidal reaches and lower freshwater reaches of larger rivers, there is often good fishing in March, April and September for slob (semi-migratory) trout averaging about 1lb (450g) and running up to 5lb (2.5kg) or more.

Daytime river fishing

Early spring fishing

Daytime river fishing is normally at its best from mid-March to early June and again in September. During the early weeks, fly fishing is totally dependent on the midday hatch of the large dark olive (*Baetis rhodani*). Outside of its emergence period, normally between 12.00 and 1.30 pm; it is difficult to gain the interest of trout.

Surprisingly, most of my early season trout are taken on a dry Hare's Ear or Greenwell. I have had little success over the years with either wet fly or nymph in March or early April. Some excellent trout can be taken on the dry fly at this time. I recall a bag of four trout, with a total weight of 6lb (2.5kg), which were taken on the dry Hare's Ear over a three-quarter-hour period on the River Bunowen, in east Galway. On the same occasion I hooked and lost a 3-4lb (1.5-2kg) fish which I found rising at the tail of a large, deep flat.

April normally brings milder weather and the trout begin to feed more actively for longer periods. The angler may use wet fly, nymph or dry fly during April, but traditionally in Ireland April is regarded as the cream of the wet-fly season. Since even the purest of Irish limestone streams are at best partially rain-fed, they only run really clear during the height of the summer. In April the rivers are often dark and flooded and the angler must depend on his sense of touch and his knowledge of the stream to give him consistent results. The ability to read the water and to know where fish are likely to lie is of inestimable value to the wet-fly angler.

If there is no apparent rise in spring, I usually fish a team of three flies, consisting of a size 10 Black and Silver on the point, a size 12 Pheasant Tail Nymph on the middle dropper, and either a size 12 or 14 Greenwell's Glory Spider or Olive Nymph on the top dropper. When the water is fining down after a flood and it has adopted that beautiful, sparkling, beer-brown colour, I often replace the mid dropper with an Orange and Grouse and the tail fly with a Red Tag. I fish my team of flies directly across the stream and mend the line immediately, allowing the flies to float motionlessly downstream. The nymphs are normally taken at this point. As the current sweeps the line around in an arc, the fish may take either the tail fly or the nymphs, and as the flies are recovered directly upstream, the tail fly is almost invariably the one which is taken. I rarely cast more than 12 to 15m but depend on a stealthy, careful approach.

Having caught a trout, do not be tempted to move on too quickly. I once took ten September trout in as many casts from a deep run on the River Bunowen. I felt a little like the character in Skues's description of Hades who, having caught six beautiful matching 2lb (1kg) trout in a row, found he was rooted to the spot and was damned for all eternity to catch the same fish from the same lie! River trout are not as easily disturbed as one would imagine and if you adopt a feline approach to stalking and land the creatures with a minimum of surface splashing, you will find the trout fully co-operative.

I have found classic upstream nymph fishing, as practised on the English chalk streams, to be of limited value in Irish limestone waters. The weighted nymph in particular is exceptionally difficult to fish in the cloudy water and one invariably finds that the movement of the main line is the first indication of a take. By the time one responds, the nymph has, nine times out of ten, been rejected by the fish. I have had limited success using a bushy dry fly, attached to a dropper some two metres along the cast, as a type of float or bite indicator. However, the whole procedure is cumbersome and takes much of the enjoyment out of using the nymph.

A unique bag of wild river brown trout (6¼lb, 5¾lb, 3¾lb, 2¾lb, 2½lb). All were taken from a midland river, in late spring, on a deep sunk nymph

Apart from their use on a cast of wet flies, my nymphs are generally reserved for those times when trout are concentrating on the hatching nymph clinging onto the surface film. Fishing for these bulging trout is really exciting, particularly when you are forced to judge solely by experience exactly where your suspended nymph is located relative to the rising trout. A cast, greased to within 2–3in (5–7.5cm) of the tail fly, good eyesight, quick reactions and short casts are all essential elements of success. Irish brown trout seem particularly fond of the nymph of the large dark olive (*Baetis rhodani*), the iron blue dun (*Baetis pumilus*), the small dark olive (*Baetis scambus*) and the yellow evening dun (*Ephemerella notata*). When feeding on the iron blue dun in late April or early May, the trout throw all caution to the wind and concentrate on the rafts of these small black-winged flies as if there will be no tomorrow. From stomach contents it is obvious that they feed indiscriminately on both duns and nymphs. However, in my experience it can be difficult at times to entice them to take a single, stationary dry fly amongst so many. A gently-twitched nymph seems to impart that added attraction and is rarely refused.

Late April/May fishing

Daytime dry-fly fishing is normally reserved for very early spring, late April, May and September. Late April/May brings the cream of the river angler's season; water temperatures are at their optimum, the trout are back in prime condition and feeding actively throughout the day. The dry-fly season commences with the iron blue dun described previously; then we see the emergence of the *Simulium* or black gnat, followed closely by the day-hatching *Hydropsyche* or grey flags, and finally we have the mayfly, *E. danica*, which emerges around 20 May. Throughout this period there may also be strong hatches of the smaller olives, such as the pale wateries (*Centroptilum luteolum*), pale evening dun (*Procloeon rufulum*) and a small dark olive (*Baetis tenax*). The dark olives often hatch on mild, blustery, showery days and can emerge in substantial numbers. If there is a cross-wind, the flies are concentrated into lines along the windward bank and invariably attract rows of trout rising practically head to tail. With the proper approach, such fish can be picked off one at a time without disturbing their brethren rising upstream. A small, size 14 Hare's Ear or Greenwell's Glory is all that is required.

September fishing

September sees a return to the olives and the pale wateries. However, the strongest rises occur to daytime-hatching blue-winged olives (*Ephemerella ignita*) and smuts. Michael Kennedy's tying of the female Blue-Winged Olive is the most successful imitation of these daytime-hatching flies. The September smuts are a mixture of *Simulium* and daytime-hatching chironomids. Trout can be very choosy when feeding on September smuts and I am convinced that poor catches are a result of anglers fishing flies which are too large rather than of the fish having a preoccupation with a particular colour. If you fish a selection of small grey dusters and green or black dry buzzers tied on size 18 to 22 hooks, you will be surprised at how dramatically your success rate improves.

Evening river fishing

Evening rises may be found on most rivers from mid-April to September. However, the most consistent and productive rises occur from May until mid-August. Evening rises in April are dependent on mild, calm conditions but can result in a period of intense if short-lived activity. The trout mainly feed on spent olives and the spinners of the iron blue dun. In May the trout are presented with an incredible array of spinners, duns, nymphs and sedges. However, in the late evenings the trout mainly concentrate on spent olives, spent gnat and the nymphs of the mayfly (*E. danica*) which may have a secondary hatch from 7.00 pm to dusk.

Although the mayfly season has often been called the duffer's fortnight, it has been my experience that the trout may become satiated with the fly after several hours' continuous feeding and the rest of the day may be spent picking at attractive morsels rather than feeding actively.

My largest river trout was one of these pickers. I was working in Ballinasloe, County Galway, at the time and having finished tagging bream on the River Suck at Derrycahill, I decided to skip dinner and to move downstream to see if I could tempt one of the legendary trout from the Bellagill area of the river. I arrived at about 7.30 pm and walked for an hour and a half without seeing a single rise. There was plenty of spent gnat about but no trout. On my arrival back at the bridge I found two locals fishing a large trout which was rising consistently to every spent gnat which came within a 6m radius. I knew that I could have had him with just one cast. I sat down adjacent to a flowering hawthorn bush and with increasing brashness dropped powerful hints that I might be given a cast, but to no avail. My colleagues were convinced that the fish would eventually take a wet fly and each of them in turn 'had a go'.

At about 9.45 I left the river and headed back to Ballinasloe and a late dinner. On crossing the Bunowen River at the Red Bridge, just outside of Ballinasloe, I got a sudden urge to stop and look for rising trout. My stomach screamed 'no!', but for once I ignored it. From the bridge, in the half darkness, I noticed tiny, gentle dimples just at the first bend in the river. I slid down the embankment and vowed to spend just five minutes before heading for food.

I took up position near the bend and watched. The minutes ticked by and nothing happened. I was just about to leave when some ten metres above me I heard a gentle smack as a trout sucked down a fly. I watched and noticed a gentle, V-shaped disturbance coming towards me. He rose again, I cast my spent gnat and waited. Nothing happened. He rose again, I cast again. Nothing happened. This scenario continued for a good four or five minutes. Then I stopped and thought. Obviously the fish was not taking spent gnat. What else could he be after? I attached a size 14 spent olive to the 4lb (2kg) leader and cast it out into the gathering darkness towards the bend in the river. I think it floated. Ever so gently the great fish moved across the pool and sipped. Was it my fly he had taken? I lifted the light rod. It literally buckled in two as he bolted for the deeper water under the bridge. For three or four long minutes he raced, jumped, burrowed and splashed. I could feel the line getting heavier as it gathered weed. Every second I expected the hook-hold to give. Eventually the fish keeled over and I bullied him into the waiting net. What a prize! — a beautifully conditioned 4½lb (2kg) wild trout. An autopsy later that evening showed that two-thirds of his stomach and his intestine were stuffed with mayfly duns. The remainder of his stomach held gnats, while the oesophagus was lined with spent olives; I have never seen such a neatly packaged lunch, tea and supper!

June sees evening rises to the spent gnat, the blue-winged olive, the yellow evening dun and an increasing array of sedges (murrough, Welshman's Button, etc). The predominant fly, however, is the blue-winged olive. This insect may hatch during the day but in general it hatches in the evening. The spinners are known as sherry spinners and these may be seen gathering in swarms from around 7.00 pm on a calm summer's evening. The female is characterised by an extruded egg sac which droops precariously below her fragile body. Great clouds of these insects may be seen to move upstream, gently dipping their abdomens in the water to release clouds of tiny adhesive eggs which quickly drop to the bottom of the stream. Once spent, the females fall on the surface of the water and they are greatly appreciated by the waiting trout. As a consequence, one often finds that fishing the blue-winged olive involves using an imitation of the spinner from 7.00 to 9.30 pm and the dun from 9.30 to 11.00.

When the yellow evening dun is hatching, the trout have a most irritating habit of taking the half-emerged dun to the exclusion of both nymph and fully-emerged dun. I have, as yet, failed to find a consistently good imitation of the half-hatched insect, and if any of my readers can enlighten me on this point, I would be delighted to hear from them.

Hatches of the blue-winged olive continue into July and early August but increasingly the hatches of evening sedge intensify so that by late July they are the dominant insect. A great variety of sedges hatch on Irish rivers (eg *Phryganea* spp., *Sericostoma personatum*, *Limnephilus* spp., *Tinodes* spp., and *Leptocerus* spp.) but in general black, brown and grey are the dominant colours. River sedges should not be fished on large-sized hooks — 10 and 12 are quite adequate.

Dry-fly techniques

Success with the dry fly is dependent on two major skills, the ability to present a motionless fly, without any perceptible drag, and the ability to stalk your prey cunningly and furtively, as this story shows.

My brother had arrived a day earlier than I on the River Shiven. We were to fish the mayfly together and that first evening I eagerly awaited his return from the river and his pronouncement on our chances for the following few days. He arrived home with three nice trout averaging about 1lb (0.5kg), but was unfortunately broken by a much larger trout — a rare occurrence for him.

The following evening we were fishing close to where he had hooked the large trout when I noticed a good fish rising in a small eddy on the far side of the river. The river was in flood and so wading was out of the question. Brendan sat patiently about 20m above me, waiting for his quarry of the previous evening to start rising. For a full hour I cast at my trout and for a full hour he refused every fly I threw at him, yet he consistently swallowed every natural that floated into the eddy. I eventually sat back and reviewed the situation. There was no doubt that my flies were dragging ever so slightly as they moved through the eddy. Could this be the cause of my problem? I decided to risk life and limb and wade out into the marginal rushes in order to gain some extra casting distance. Having carefully waded out, I waited until the fish had taken two more natural duns. I then overcast the eddy and, as the fly was about to alight on the far bank, I jerked back on the line and set the mayfly amongst some loose coils of nylon at the head of the eddy. Gently, my fly floated through the eddy, pulling the loose coils of nylon after it. My main leader swung around the perimeter of the eddy, in the main current. Just as the main line was about to exert maximum pull on the cast and thus drag the fly, the trout rose. I tightened and he was mine. The fish was larger than I expected, a good 2½lb (1kg) but, even more surprisingly, it had two mayflies in its jaw; one of which was attached to 12in (30cm) of freshly broken nylon!

EQUIPMENT

Rods

My own preference is for an 8½ft (2.5m), medium-action fly rod, which can double as either a wet-fly/nymph or dry-fly rod. I also use a 7ft (2m) brook rod, which has a stiffer action than the 8½ft rod but is ideal for small enclosed rivers and streams.

Reels

I would advise a simple 3in (7.5cm) reel with a strong ratchet. It should be capable of taking a size 4 to 7 double-tapered line and some 50m of strong, braided, nylon backing.

Lines

Lines should, of course, match the rod, but I prefer a size 5 double-tapered on my small brook rod and a 6 or 7 double-tapered on the larger rod.

Leaders (Casts)

For river fishing it is essential to use a tapered cast. My river version consists of: 1½ft of 12–15lb, 4–6ft of 8lb, 3ft of 6lb, 3ft of 4lb (45cm of 5.5-6.5kg, 1–2m of 3.5kg, 1m of 2.5kg, 1m of 2kg). For the brook rod the lengths are scaled down to: 1½ft of 12lb, 1½ft of 8lb, 1½ft of 6lb, 3ft of 4lb (45cm of 5.5kg, 45cm of 3.5kg, 45cm of 2.5kg, 1m of 2kg). There are also good quality knotless, tapered casts now available commercially but they are expensive. Droppers should be 3-4in (7.5-10cm) long and should stand out from the cast. When sedge or mayfly fishing, I always use a terminal section of 6-8lb (2.5-3.5kg) nylon; otherwise you will find that these larger flies are easily cracked off when casting. For fishing really low clearwater streams with smuts or other small dry fly, I do occasionally use 3lb (1.5kg) nylon, but never anything less than this.

Net

I always use a home-made 16in (40cm) diameter net with a light frame and a light 36in (90cm) handle made from hollow plastic tubing. A shorter 24in (60cm) handle will suffice, but when fishing drained or heavily-weeded rivers, the long-handled version has considerable advantages.

Waders

Thigh waders are an essential item of equipment. However, when fishing even-bottomed rivers, such as the River Suir, body waders can be of great advantage. But remember, they are heavy and cumbersome and definitely not conducive to walking several kilometres!

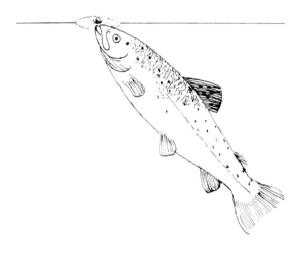

111

BROWN TROUT FISHING TECHNIQUES

It is far from what one would consider an idyllic May day. There is a strong, cool, westerly wind forcing the white, blossom-laden May bushes to bend and sway precariously. Much of the early blossom has disappeared from the branches and its remains are dotted about amongst the yellow furze and the bankside sedges. It is 10.30 am and we are embarking on our first day's mayfly fishing of the season on the River Shiven. From past experience we know it will be at least 12.00 pm before there is any appreciable hatch of 'fly'. Still, it is exciting to see the odd large dun sail past, its great sail wings erect, looking incongruous against the size of the stream.

We decide to fish different areas of the river and to meet at lunchtime to compare notes. I make my way towards Rookhill, some 3km above Ballinamore Bridge, where I have dropped my brother, Brendan. As I tackle up I scan the river for signs of rising fish, but apart from the odd parr splashing at a passing morsel, the river is dead. This is nothing new, for river fishing is mainly a matter of patience and faith. I walk some 200m upstream and choose a large limestone flag as a throne. I wait and watch. Just above me the river takes a sharp left bend and its banks are covered in a dense mass of trees and shrubs. The river here is an even glide, harbouring dense stands of *Ranunculus*. Ideal *Simulium* country. As the morning wears on, the dense clouds of small black flies begin to gather and as their numbers increase so does their eagerness and activity. The gusting wind blows the clouds near to the water's surface and small clumps of struggling black flies are marooned in the surface film. The trout start to rise eagerly. Several small fish at first, but eventually some larger fish appear in the corner pool. Within an hour and a half I have landed six trout and hooked as many more. All are below 1lb

(0.5kg) and are carefully returned to the water. They have taken a small, plain, size 16, black-bodied, black-hackled fly.

During the sixties we consistently fished the River Blackwater in County Meath and grew to know and love that beautiful river. However, we made one fatal mistake. We fished only the faster pools and runs which held prodigious quantities of 6oz to 1¼lb (170-570g) fish, but few bigger. One season, before the river was so cruelly drained, on the advice of our good friend, Ned Cusack, my brother and I decided to abandon the flows and hunt the deeper slow-flowing pools. What a day we had! I initially lost a 4lb+ (2kg) trout on a lake-sized duckfly (the only black fly in my box!) which was feeding in a leisurely manner on black gnat. A frisky bullock attempted to butt me as I netted the fish. I jerked the rod with fright and pulled out of the mighty trout. However, we later captured, on the mayfly, two trout of 2½ and 2¾lb (1-1.5kg) and six others between 1 and 1½lb (450-680g). Ever since, our mayfly motto has been 'abandon the flows'.

But back on the Shiven, it is 12.30 pm and time to abandon the flows and head for the deeper water. I walk downstream towards the head of the deeper pools above Ballinamore Bridge. In the distance I can see Brendan astride a stile, patiently waiting. Not a great sign. I adopt a similar strategy, but facing downstream. After a few minutes' observation I have seen no less than four trout feeding near to my perch. They are all making that characteristic slashing rise which is so much a part of daytime sedge fishing. I walk inland for some 30m or more and move downstream. I work my way in towards the bank at the head of some faster water but below the pool. I sink down on one knee and watch. Sure enough, I notice some grey flags in the air above the water; their characteristic roof-shaped wings and scuttering flight pattern make them easy to identify. I attach a size 10 Brown Sedge to the cast and cover the first fish. For an hour the sport continues, but this section is quite exposed to the strong wind and it is difficult to cover the fish. Nevertheless, I take two, one of which is 1¼lb (570g). Brendan joins me for lunch. He has had a quiet morning and has only taken three trout, all of which he returned. However, he did see some mayfly in the lower pools and spotted an exceptionally large 4-6lb (2-2.5kg) fish which tantalised him by rising only twice during the whole morning.

Following lunch we again separate. I move downstream but Brendan decides to remain at Ballinamore. I motor down to Islandcausk and proceed slowly upstream. The first 100m or so above the bridge is canopied by large ash and willow trees. Black gnat are present in huge swarms and their constant drone and buzz can be heard even from the road bridge. Smaller trout are feeding avidly on the black feast. Despite a strong temptation to take *just* one cast, I move on towards the first deep corner pool.

There are two trout rising, one fish just above the fast water and a second much larger fish in the main pool itself. The larger fish is moving freely about, picking off every nymph and mayfly he can find. I know that I must take out the smaller trout to prevent him bolting upstream and alarming his larger colleague. I cast towards the trout but my attention is deflected by a great splash upstream; the lower trout takes but my reaction is too slow and I merely prick the fish. He splashes on the surface and bolts — thankfully downstream. Have I disturbed the other fish? I sink into the heavy bankside vegetation and wait. Initially the fish rises intermittently, obviously aware of the encounter downstream. But after five minutes he is back feeding avidly. With my heart pounding, I cast towards the fish and wait. My great dry mayfly drifts downstream, perfectly placed. Nothing happens until the fly is directly opposite to me. Suddenly, I see the fish actually follow the fly

downstream. Just as it reaches the lip of the pool, the trout lunges forward and sips down the fly. The fish turns, I lift the rod and he races forward into the centre of the pool, thrashing his great head from side to side. For several minutes he thrashes and dashes about but he is quite confined in the pool. Just when I think he is tiring the fish gives a strong lunge. My fingers, which are acting as a governor on the line, slip and the fish is stuck solid in a weedbed. I point the rod at the trout and tap the butt to irritate the hook-hold, but to no avail. I can see the shape moving in the weedbed for several minutes, but eventually he disappears. My 3lb (1.5kg) trout is gone!

Despondent, I move on upstream, but the hatch has petered out and even the black gnat are less abundant. I walk back to the car and make a refreshing cup of tea.

On returning to Ballinamore Bridge, I regale Brendan with the tale of my great lost trout, but he too has had his troubles, for soon after I left him the rise died completely and he has not seen a fish rise in more than two hours. However, fishing a 15ft (4.5m) leader and a weighted mayfly nymph, he has managed to take two good trout — both over 1lb (450g) in weight.

At around 6.00 pm the wind begins to wane and the mayflies return. By 7.00 pm there is a really strong hatch of fly and the moderate breeze has concentrated them into a small, calm area near a high clay bank. Taking it in turns, we fish this area carefully and for almost an hour are rewarded with fish after fish. When the rise finally subsides we compare notes and find that we have taken some fourteen fish in the hour, three of which we retained. All were over 1lb (450g) in weight, the biggest being 1lb 10oz (740g). It is now after 8.00 pm and beginning to get quite cold. We decide that there is little prospect of an evening rise, so we return to the hotel, well satisfied with our day's sport.

Alternative angling methods

I am sure that there are those amongst you who well remember the heady days of the fifties and sixties when trout abounded in our rivers, angling pressure was low to non-existent (even in our city rivers) and angling clubs patiently tolerated the antics of their juvenile, bait-fishing members, such as myself, who, it was assumed, would 'come right' (ie turn to fly fishing) in the end. I could regale you with stories of fishing the live minnow, using Asprin bottle tops as floats, or free-lining the poor creatures in the white, foamy waters of weirs and waterfalls. I could tell you of the antics of the trout as they chased the suspended minnow round and round the cork float before finally rising to the bait at the surface. But alas, live baiting is now banned and gone forever. However cruel, however unfeeling it may have been, I cannot find it in myself to regret my experiences; for they were intimately entwined with the happiest and most carefree of city childhoods.

Worm

Brown trout are very fond of earthworms and will take them under almost all weather and water conditions. Most anglers start their fishing careers using a humble worm, spinning rod and reel and a stout lump of lead. It is unfortunate that the majority become quickly disillusioned with their poor catches and switch to either spinning or fly fishing. They retain an image of worm fishing for trout as a crude, uninteresting pastime which should be greatly discouraged. They also, for some strange reason, quickly forget the reason they initially rejected the technique and are loud in their condemnation of the worm's ability to strip a river clear of trout.

In the hands of the skilled proponent of the art, there is no more delicate or gentle way of catching trout. It is quite extraordinary to note how often the truly skilled dry-fly fisherman is attracted to, and equally skilled with, the classic upstream worm. I can think of three excellent river trout anglers who fit this description: Pat Conneff, that well-known Dublin angler, my brother Brendan, and the late Pat O'Brien, who died tragically in the late 1960s. Of the three, Pat O'Brien had the true Midas touch. Fishing an 8½ft (2.5m) hardy split-cane rod, a cheap metal fly reel and a green, level Kingfisher line, he would stalk the runs, flows, eddies and weirpools of our native River Dodder. Using a 6ft (2m) length of 3lb (1.5kg) nylon as a cast, a simple Pennell tackle of two size 12 hooks, and fishing no more than 3m of line and cast combined, he would winkle out trout after trout from the most unlikely pools and eddies. Ever aware of the damage which his skills could inflict on any given pool, he returned most of his lip-hooked trout unharmed to the water — and 99 per cent of his trout were so hooked. Wading deep, while holding the rod high and fishing directly upstream, he could sense the least tweak on his line. He was fastidious regarding the addition of lead-shot and his line was weighted according to conditions; never more than four, never less than one (BB) shot. That worm had to tumble along the bottom in the most natural way possible.

Brown trout may also be taken on the legered worm, the float-fished worm, and even at times on a spun worm! The methods used are similar to those described for sea trout and salmon. Brown trout prefer brandlings and red-headed worms to blackheads or lobworms. Also, one should remember to fish relatively small worms, for trout seem to prefer these. When worm fishing in fast water, be extra careful to strike at every bite, for salmon and trout parr are greatly attracted to the bait and if given half a chance will gobble down an amazingly large portion.

Corr bait

This is an excellent bait but is limited in its distribution. Basically it is caddis fly larvae which are gathered in their cases from under stones or other stream debris. The caddis in the small, pebble-lined cases (*Limnephilus* spp.) are a particularly good bait. They may be stored in a small container of water and left in their cases until just before use. They are normally float-fished on a fly rod using a fixed-spool reel of 3-5lb (1.5-2.5kg) nylon. Two corr bait are removed from their cases and placed on a size 10 or 12 hook, depending on the size of the larvae, and the float is rigged so that the bait floats just above the bottom. The hook is passed through the thorax but the creatures are very soft and fall off quite easily. These are superb bait, at times, particularly during early summer evenings when the river is low.

Spinning

I have seen brown trout taken on every imaginable spinner, from mackerel spinners to pike plugs, but in general it is either the Mepps or Devon which is most often used. Except in really high water conditions, it is generally unnecessary to use any lead. I normally fish a main line of 6-8lb (2.5-3.5kg), then a size 8 swivel and a 1m cast of 4-6lb (2-2.5kg) nylon. I prefer either a small size 0 or 1 copper Mepps or a 1-2in (2.5-5cm) blue and silver Devon. Lane minnows are also excellent baits, as are very small Tobys. I invariably fish across and downstream and, as in the case of sea trout, I tend to consistently alter the pace of the retrieve. I am also a great believer in letting the flow of the river do most of the work for me. If trout are following the bait, remember the trick mentioned previously of stopping the retrieve and allowing the bait to flutter towards the bottom.

Natural minnow

Large spawning shoals of minnow tend to gather in shallow water during the months of June and July. Outside of this period they prefer the more slow-flowing reaches. Locating minnow shoals will normally involve a reconnaissance, for ideally you require minnow of 1½-2½in (4-6.5cm).

I normally use a minnow trap fashioned from an old brandy bottle to capture my bait. To make the trap, tap the inverted 'duck end' of the bottle with a sharp pointed instrument until you have formed a 1in (2.5cm) diameter hole; finally, loosely plug the neck of the trap with grass.

Trapping and killing minnow
Break a slice of white or brown crumbly bread into small pieces and place inside the bottle. Fill the bottle carefully with water by immersing the neck and allowing water to flow into the 'duck end'. When full, either let it roll away from you down under the bank or, if the ledge is some distance out, push the attached cord of the bottle with a fork stick. Watch out for clouds of mud as the bottle settles, for there is little point in leaving the bottle where it is immersed in soft mud. If there are minnow about, they will quickly gather around the bottle and may be clearly seen against the white bread pieces. If no minnow appear within four or five minutes, move to a neighbouring location. When minnow enter the bottle, you will see the bread moving. Leave it for ten minutes or so and then carefully retrieve the bottle. Do not leave it for any great length of time as the minnow will eventually find their way back out. Put the palm of your hand over the top of the bottle, lift it over your container and remove the grass stopper, thus releasing the minnow into the waiting bucket. I much prefer freshly killed minnow, but there is now legislation banning the transportation of live fish, so you must kill your minnow before transporting them. To kill them, simply hold them between finger and thumb in one hand and give a flick on the back of the head with the index finger of the other hand. If you intend to use them immediately, store them in damp grass or damp paper. Do not store dead minnow in water, as they quickly soften and begin to decompose. Deep freezing is the best method for long-term preservation.

Fishing the minnow
The dead minnow may be either legered or darted. The leger method can be very effective at times but has the disadvantage of attracting eels. To leger a minnow, simply sow a size 10 hook through the lips, back and tail of the fish. Either a running or fixed leger may be used.

The quantity of lead used may be varied depending on conditions, but the hook sizes (a size 12 single and a size 16 treble) should be kept constant. There is a great deal of pressure on the knot joining the single hook to the line and it may be necessary to replace the trace several times during the day. Always check this joint for wear after a fish has been landed.

Choose a minnow approximately 2in (5cm) long and insert the single through the two lips. Place the treble along the minnow's flank, just behind the dorsal fin. It is imperative that a slight bend is put in the fish before embedding in the treble, for the degree of this bend regulates the wobble

The rewards of deep trolling. A brace of ten-pounders for Des Elliot from L. Mask, Co. Mayo

or darting movement of the bait. Cast the bait directly across the stream and retrieve it using a basic sink-and-draw action, but with the addition of a distinct twitching movement of the rod tip between each draw.

The actual speed of retrieval may be varied depending on water height. Under low flow conditions even rising trout will race after the minnow if it is darted a metre or so in front of them. When minnow are in full spawning livery, choose only the black-backed, silver-bellied, females. (The multicoloured males are next to useless for darting.) Pregnant female minnow can prove almost irresistible to trout.

Fishing the minnow has given me a lot of pleasure but it may be used to excess and in ruthless hands is one of the few angling methods capable of doing serious damage to river trout stocks. In contrast, the fish are normally lip-hooked and may easily be returned to the water. Fished sparingly it can prove a great novelty.

Trolling

There are two distinct types of trolling carried out on Irish lakes. There is the early season mid-water trolling of Lane minnows and Mepps, when the fish are feeding on sticklebacks, snails or crustaceans, and true deep-water trolling for large ferox trout in the great western lakes. Deep-water trolling involves the use of echo-sounders, downriggers, rod holders, etc, and is more akin to pike trolling. The large ferox fish range in weight from 8 to 20lb (3.5–9kg) or more and are normally taken on large spoons or Devons.

Mid-water trolling mainly takes place from February to the end of April and again during calm, warm conditions in midsummer. The rig is the same as that used for spring salmon spinning except that the weight is varied depending on the depth being fished, and the baits used are substantially smaller. In Lough Owel near Mullingar, County Westmeath, there is a strong local tradition of spring trolling. The anglers use either a 2–3in (5–7.5cm) Lane minnow or a size 2 gold or silver Mepps. In late March they normally fish a lure with a splash of red or orange, for at this time the sticklebacks have built their nests and the males have taken on their vivid spawning livery. Trolling in midsummer is a good deal less successful but the angler could be fortunate enough to pick up the odd really good 3lb+ perch!

CHAPTER 5

RAINBOW TROUT

Origin

Life cycle and biology

Rainbow trout (*Salmo gairdneri*) are native to the coastal drainage area of North America, extending from Alaska southward to Mexico. There are two distinct strains of rainbow trout, the steelhead or migratory form, which in many ways is analogous to the Atlantic salmon, both in its migration pattern and behaviour on return to fresh water and in the resident, non-migratory form. As in the case of brown trout, the nomenclature of rainbow trout originally included other Latin names such as *Salmo irideus* and *Salmo irideus shasta*; the former, *S. irideus*, was considered the typical form of rainbow which came from the coastal streams of California, while *S. i. shasta* came from the Sierra Nevada streams south of Mount Shasta, the best known of which is the McCloud River.

More recently two North American scientists have claimed that the rainbow trout is more closely related to Pacific salmon (*Oncorhynchus*) than to the brown trout and Atlantic salmon (*Salmo*). They have therefore proposed that the rainbow's scientific name should be changed to *Oncorhychus mykiss*.

Spawning

All rainbow trout, including steelheads, spawn in spring. Natural spawning can occur at any time from February to May, but it is usual for rainbows to spawn in late March or April. However, the *shasta* form is known to spawn in very early spring and, when domesticated, careful broodstock selection can ensure spawning as early as November. Confusion has arisen over this point and it has often been stated that there are two distinct strains of rainbow trout; one a spring spawner (*irideus*) and one an autumn spawner (*shasta*). This does not seem to be the case, for when released into the wild, the *shasta* strain quickly revert to early spring spawning. This has serious implications for the fishery manager, since spring spawning trout may be in poor conditions (particularly the males) well into late May or early June. Where natural spawning occurs, angling seasons must therefore be regulated accordingly.

Although it occurs in spring, the actual spawning act of the rainbow trout is similar in every way to that of the brown trout, the result being a redd into which the eggs are laid and covered with small stones. Spring spawning in Irish spate rivers would be a most precarious procedure, biologically, since the eggs would most likely be left high and dry long before they hatched.

Fast-growing fish

Given suitable conditions, rainbow trout are exceptionally fast growing, early maturing fish. They normally first spawn at two to three years of age but some males mature at one year old. They are a short-lived fish and rarely survive more than five or six seasons. They are prodigious feeders and will continue to forage actively even during the hottest summer weather. Unlike brown trout, they do, at times, feed on vegetable matter, and while they are browsing on plant material their flesh may become tainted and muddy to the taste; this normally happens during warm weather in July and August.

The fastest-growing Irish rainbow trout are to found in Lough Acalla, near Ballinasloe, County Galway. This is a small, 30 acre (12ha) lake situated in a carboniferous limestone depression. It is an extremely rich and productive water, holding a phenomenal density of invertebrate fauna, particularly shrimp (*Gammarus*), on which the trout feed extensively. The deepest area in the lake is no more than 2.5m and its clear, spring-fed water ensures maximum plant growth. Rainbows stocked into the lake in April or May at 3–4oz (80–120g) can reach 3–4lb (1.5–2kg) within fourteen to sixteen months. In recent years the lake has been stocked with a mixture of one- and two-year-old rainbows. These have not survived as well as the fish which were formerly stocked as summerlings or fry. They are often ugly, fin-damaged creatures and have not the same fine lines and light silver coloration of the trout stocked at a younger age. A reversion to the former stocking regime would greatly improve both the over-wintering rate and the quality of the stock.

MacCrimmon, who published an excellent paper on the worldwide distribution of rainbow trout in 1971, observes that the range of 12°C to 20°C is considered to be optimum for the species and that they can withstand higher temperature regimes than brown trout. He further comments: 'Water temperatures where the species makes a worthwhile contribution to local fisheries within the native and introduced range generally approach 15°–20°C for prolonged periods each year.' He quotes workers who say that feeding is negligible below 5°C and above 25°C.

Stocks and management

Introduction into Ireland

The first successful importation of rainbow trout eggs into England and Scotland from the United States occurred in 1885. From 1888 to 1905 shipments of ova or fry were made practically every winter to one or more hatcheries in Britain and Ireland. The original introductions into Ireland took place in 1899, 1900 and 1901. The earlier shipments into Britain probably consisted of pure *shasta* strain from the McCloud River. Subsequent importations comprised either *Salmo irideus* or the hybridised type resulting from a mixture of the two. While no steelhead rainbows were introduced into Britain from the United States, some steelhead blood may have been introduced through the purchase of ova from Europe, where they had been introduced into continental hatcheries. In latter years various new strains and crosses of rainbow trout have developed in order to fulfil the requirements of the ever-expanding aquaculture industry. In Ireland, at least, such strains have not been purposefully stocked into the wild although some major escapements from marine cages have occurred.

Present stocks

Since rainbow trout are exceptionally fast growing, easily domesticated and relatively cheap to produce, they have become very popular in fisheries which are dependent on artificial stocks to maintain good angling. Despite the fact that they have now been stocked into many thousands of waters, both river and lake, over the past 100 years, it is interesting to note that in only five waters in Britain and Ireland have self-sustaining populations developed and in only one of these is the population maintained without annual stocking. There are records from about forty localities of rainbows reproducing (fish spawning, eggs identified, even young 1+ trout produced), but apparently these reproductive activities do not result in the establishment of self-maintained populations. In Ireland there are records of rainbow trout reproducing on Lough Shure on Arranmore Island off County Donegal, Lough na Leibe, County Sligo, and White Lake, County Westmeath. However, Lough Shure is the only location where a fully self-maintaining population is present.

In the fifty years from 1905 to 1955, no further rainbow trout were imported into Ireland. The Inland Fisheries Trust imported ova and fry from Great Britain in 1955 and these formed the basis of the present brood stock which is held at Fannure fish farm, Roscrea, County Tipperary. Fish from this hatchery have now been stocked into several hundred waters, both rivers and lakes. Originally, stocking was confined to fry or fingerlings but in latter years the demand for put-and-take fishing has increased, particularly from tourist areas such as West Cork and Kerry, and as a result rainbows are now stocked as either yearlings or two-year-olds.

In Northern Ireland the demand for stocked rainbow trout has grown even more rapidly and waters stocked with rainbows, from the government-owned Movanagher fish farm, are widely spread throughout the province.

Varying levels of success

The view has long been held in Ireland that if rainbow trout were stocked into a water which has access to the sea or other larger systems, they would quickly disappear, since their migratory instincts would impel them downstream. Our Irish rainbows have little if any innate migratory instincts, and the disappearance of stocked fish has a number of possible explanations. The fish may be dying off, either due to competition from resident fish or to their inability to adapt to natural food, or it may be that they are showing the same limited propensity to wander as stocked brown trout which have not been imprinted on a given water. Surprisingly, all the evidence gathered to date would suggest that, even in riverine situations, loss of stocked rainbows by migration is negligible.

Where large one+ or two-year-old rainbows are stocked into lakes holding small or medium wild brown trout, concern has been expressed regarding the effects of the larger implants on the resident community, particularly in terms of their availability to the angler. Circumstantial evidence suggests that resident trout will attempt to harass and displace all other planted trout, even those larger than themselves. In such situations it is not surprising to find that the more active, stressed residents figure less frequently in the angler's bag than heretofore — they are in essence too busy defending their patch to bother with the delectable surface or sub-surface morsels offered by the angler. In such waters, however, the decision to stock would not have been taken had the natural fishery provided adequate angling and the resultant drop in the numbers of wild trout is generally of little consequence.

Where rainbow trout are introduced into rich virgin waters, they can do exceptionally well. I have mentioned earlier the extraordinary growth rates achieved in Lough Acalla, County Galway, but it is my contention that we are far too conservative regarding the use of rainbow trout in our fisheries. By stocking fish as fry or yearlings, one may produce a full-finned trout to rival the most handsome of wild rainbows. There is a world of difference between the finless stockie of the English reservoirs, which is generally caught within six weeks of planting, and the fish which has grown naturally for one, two or even three years. Given the techniques which are now available to monitor the appearance of weak year-classes, I would suggest that, in suitable fisheries (such as Lough Owel, County Westmeath), serious consideration should be given to plugging such population gaps with fry, fingerling or yearling rainbows. I know that they will be acceptable to most anglers and I am convinced that even the sceptics will change their tune when they first encounter the savage take and heart-stopping acrobatics of a naturalised four-pounder!

This suggestion is not new, for even in the early 1970s Winifred Frost of the Freshwater Biological Association, Windermere, stated:

Fortunately man can control the number of rainbows because it is so very rarely that a rainbow establishes a population. Therefore if it is for any reason desirable to have them reduced or eliminated from a water this can be done, there being no fear of future recruitment. This almost 'inability' to create populations may be regarded as a safeguard against the rainbow gaining supremacy over the brown trout provided man wisely manages the stocking of the rainbows in these waters.

Another radical suggestion would be the use of sea-reared rainbows in put-and-take fisheries, particularly those near the coast. Some of these fish are of the most excellent quality, with firm palatable flesh, full fins and a beautiful silver coating broken only by that characteristic magenta flush along their flanks. I am sure they would make the most magnificent sport fish, particularly if they could be planted into a sluice-operated or boomed sea lough.

In addition, silver flanked, all female (triploid) rainbows can now be produced quite readily. These fish grow fast, retain condition throughout the winter months and provide the fishery manager with an ideal late autumn or winter stock.

I am a totally incurable rainbow addict. From my first encounter with these wonderful trout in the early sixties, I have fished most of the stocked waters in Ireland and even ventured further afield to fish for wild rainbows in the rivers and lakes of mid-west and western Canada. But Lough Acalla is the rainbow water which I know best and my comments on tackling naturalised rainbows are primarily based on experiences gained from this water over the past twenty-five years.

Put-and-take fisheries

Early season fishing
The majority of Irish lakes that are stocked with rainbows do not open before May or June. However, I have had limited experience of fishing for stocked rainbows in a relatively poor series of lakes during March and April. The lakes I fished were in fact reservoirs situated in the Dublin mountains. Because of their location there is often snow on the ground in early March and water temperatures hover between 1°C and 6°C for most of the month. When stocked into really cold water, rainbows can be exceptionally dour and seem to lack any incentive to shoal or feed. They remind me in many ways of spring salmon, lying almost comatose in the cold spring water.

However, even the briefest of mild spells will bring about a dramatic change in behaviour; the fish seem to form great heterogeneous shoals, holding fish of all sizes. These roam about the lake searching for food and seem principally interested in surface insects. They are easy prey to a sub-surface lure such as a Baby Doll or an Appetiser — especially if it is fished on a floating line and leaves a clearly discernible wake. One of the most extraordinary features of early season fishing for freshly stocked rainbows is the fact that the disturbance of landing fish actually attracts other trout to the area. One will often see half a dozen or more fish swirling and gadding about in the vicinity of hooked fish. I believe that the fish associate surface activity with feeding rather than danger and imagine that the unfortunate hooked fish is having the feed of his life!

I remember on one occasion taking twelve rainbows up to 3lb (1.5kg) in quick succession before

123

having to leave the 'hotspot' because of a luncheon appointment. All but one of the fish were released and even this did not deter the trout's enthusiasm for my Appetiser. As I waded ashore, a friend of mine, who had been watching the performance for some time, replaced me on the point of the rocky promontory where I had been fishing. While packing my car I noticed, to my surprise, that he had not encountered a single fish. I later learned that he had thrashed the area for a full hour before catching his first rainbow. Five more followed in quick succession and he had a similar experience to my own, with great swirls and splashes accompanying each hooked fish to the net. It seems that in the time it took me to wade ashore and my friend to replace me that the shoal had lost interest in the area and moved on. He then had to wait a further hour until the shoal mooched by on their return journey.

By mid-April these early season stockies will have come to terms with their new environment and will be feeding mainly on bottom organisms such as snails, caddis and, if they are present, shrimp. To fish for these bottom feeders I would normally use a sinking line and either a Black Chenille, Appetiser or Baby Doll. Line density is dependent on the water which you are fishing; if it is a deep, steep-shelving reservoir, a fast-sinking shooting head might be best but a slow or moderately-fast sinking line may be more appropriate for shallower, natural lakes or ponds. If the fish are feeding on cased caddis larvae, there is no better imitation than a Stick Fly twitched slowly along the bottom.

May onwards

In those fisheries where takable fish are stocked in May or early June (eg Pallas or White Lake), you will find that the fish are relatively free-rising and easy to catch for the first week or so. However, if there is surface food about (eg hatches of olives or chironomids), the fish become selective quite quickly. They are not as discerning as wild browns or naturalised rainbows and will take a general imitation rather than requiring an almost exact replica of the hatching insect. A cast containing a general olive and chironomid imitation will suffice, provided they represent the appropriate stage on which the fish are feeding (ie nymph, adult or pupa). Even at this point in the season some trout may be enticed to a surface lure and the ardent lure fisherman will continue to take fish, though not in the same numbers as he did during the first week. He will also lose a great deal of the enjoyment if he fails to change to a more imitative form of fishing.

A family treat

Many of the smaller put-and-take fisheries are located in areas where natural trout-feeding is poor. Therefore, the stocked fish are continuously hungry and as a consequence are readily taken by the angler. In situations such as these, exploitation rates of 80 to 90 per cent are not uncommon.

If tastefully stocked with a quasi-natural size range of trout, which are not out of proportion with either the size of the water or the natural expectations of the angler, then put-and-take fisheries are to be welcomed. They provide the family angler with a location where even children can really enjoy a day's angling without all of the planning and paraphernalia which goes into a serious session. They give the youngsters the chance to catch a decent fish on the fly and provide that added incentive which hopefully will result in a lifelong interest in angling. For the dedicated, serious angler (yes, they too appear on such waters, despite their denials and protestations), they provide a haven during unseasonable weather, where flagging spirits may be uplifted and a brace or two of trout taken with relative ease.

Naturalised rainbows

Within six to eight weeks of being stocked into a rich fishery, rainbows will have adapted to the water and the natural feeding regime. The one- and two-year-old fish will have formed homogeneous shoals and the larger, over-wintered rainbows will be found moving about singly or in small groups. Feeding will follow a pattern similar to that described for brown trout in small limestone lakes. Rainbows, however, have certain preferences for key insects and organisms and so I propose to move quickly through the season on typical stillwater fishing, outlining some of the rainbow's peculiarities.

Early summer fishing

When fishing in May you will encounter both freshly stocked trout and fish which have been in the lake for one, two or occasionally three years. The naturalised fish will be feeding principally on snails, sedge pupae, olive nymphs and adults. Later in the month some of the larger sedges will appear and these may bring on a short but intense evening rise.

In June the rainbows really come to the surface and if insects are hatching they will rise throughout the day. They have a great liking for chironomid pupae and will, at times, rise to tiny individuals even during the hottest period of the day. Such rises will continue well into July and August.

June also sees the emergence of the murrough or great red sedge. These great roof-winged creatures hatch in open water and then scutter across the surface towards the shore. Rainbows love these insects and will at times throw all caution to the wind and chase them right into the shallows. This is an opportunity to fish a dry artificial which will cause a distinctive wake as you slowly and erratically twitch it across the surface. You should be warned that the rainbows will take the murrough with a savage lunge and if there is a chance of a really big fish (4lb+; 2kg) the use of an 8–10lb (3.5–4.5kg) leader is more than justified.

The fisherman's curse or *Caenis* also emerges in June. This fly hatches in prodigious numbers and the fish love to cruise around the surface, feeding on rafts of the emerging insects. At such times I have found that a large lure stripped through the shoals of feeding fish is the angler's only real hope, for although it is possible to imitate the individual insect, it is impossible to imitate the rafts or clumps. However, when the spinners return to lay their eggs, around dusk, fish may be taken using a single, dry, size 16 Spent Olive. Various forms of buzzer also hatch in the late evening and a strong hatch can continue well after dusk.

Midsummer fishing

July and August see a diminution in the degree of daytime surface activity. However, at times the smaller rainbows may become totally preoccupied with the midday buzzer hatch. Sedge hatches reach their peak, and although the murrough has disappeared by mid-July, it is replaced by a myriad of brown and black sedges, principally silver horns and *Limnephilids*.

In Lough Acalla, during August, a medium-sized black buzzer hatches during the day. The pupae are scarlet in colour and a size 12 Scarlet and Mallard is an excellent imitation of the hatching insect. It prefers mild, wet, windy conditions and at times its emergence brings on a strong rise of trout. As I mentioned previously, rainbows may feed on vegetation during July and August which may taint their flesh. If such is the case, return all fish until September when they will have reverted exclusively to an invertebrate diet.

Autumn fishing

The September/October period sees a return to daytime fishing. Shrimp numbers have by this time greatly increased and they have reached a large and acceptable size. Rainbows may be found feeding extensively amongst the stones and boulders of the more exposed shores. They will readily take either a shrimp imitation or a Wickham's. I have also found that Watson's Fancy is a firm favourite with these shrimp-feeding fish on dark stormy days. The larger fish also become more aggressive at this time and both surface and mid-water lures do well.

Some idiosyncrasies

There are two areas where Irish rainbows seem to differ from their British counterparts. Firstly, they do not appear to indulge in the so called 'orange madness' which is so prevalent in the richer English reservoirs during July. At this time the rainbows feed extensively on planktonic blooms — particularly *Daphnia* — and are insanely attracted to orange lures. Although Irish rainbows do feed on summer plankton, they display little preference for orange above any other colour in a lure. It is also exceptionally rare for Irish rainbows to take 'on the drop'. This may be due to the relative shallowness of the Irish lakes or to the more coloured nature of the water, particularly in rain-fed catchments.

Alternative angling methods

Freshly stocked rainbows fall easy prey to an attractively presented worm. Many of the techniques described for sea trout and brown trout will also catch rainbows but there is little sport in taking stocked fish on worms.

Even for novices, the bubble float (see page 85) or spinning are far more attractive ways of catching rainbows. As in the case of sea trout, the wake of the bubble seems to attract rainbows and they will often follow the float and not the attached lure into shallow water. Rainbows prefer bright, flashy spinning lures and some of the most gaudy concoctions can be amazingly effective. The advantage of the bubble and the spinner is that fish may be released unharmed, whereas in the case of the worm, the rainbows are invariably hooked in the back of the throat.

L. na Léibe, Co. Sligo, one of the few Irish waters in which rainbows have been known to spawn

APPENDIX 1
Fly dressings

SALMON FLIES (SPRING)

Willie Gunn
Body: Black floss ribbed with wide oval gold tinsel.
Wing: Orange bucktail under yellow bucktail under black bucktail, tied all round.
Tube: Brass or aluminium 1–2½in (2.5–6cm) long.

Garry Dog
Body: Black floss ribbed with flat silver tinsel.
Wing: Alternating bunches of red and yellow bucktail — two of each.
Tube: Brass or aluminium 1–2½in (2.5–6cm) long.

SALMON FLIES (SPRING AND SUMMER)

Thunder and Lightning
Body: Black floss ribbed with oval gold.
Hackle: Orange cock with blue jay or dyed blue gallina throat hackle.
Wing: Bronze mallard with topping over and jungle cock cheeks.
Tag: Oval silver tinsel and yellow floss.
Butt: Black ostrich herl.
Tail: Topping and Indian crow substitute.
Hook: Sizes 2 to 8, single or double.

Munro Killer
Body: Black floss ribbed with oval gold.
Hackle: Orange cock or blue jay under dyed blue gallina.
Wing: Yellow bucktail under black bucktail.
Tag: Oval gold.
Hook: Sizes 2 to 8, single or double; 4 to 10 treble.

Silver Doctor
Body: Flat silver tinsel ribbed with oval silver.
Throat: Kingfisher-blue dyed hackle under fibres of widgeon.
Wing: Mixed: tippet in strands with strips of golden pheasant tail over 'married' strands of scarlet, blue and yellow swan; strips of teal and grey mallard; narrow strips of bronze mallard over; a topping over all and jungle cock cheeks.
Head: Red varnish.
Tag: Fine oval silver and golden yellow floss.
Butt: Red wool.
Tail: A topping and kingfisher-blue hackle points.
Hook: Sizes 2 to 8 single; 10 double.

Hairy Mary
Body: Black floss ribbed with oval gold.
Throat: Blue cock.
Wing: Brown bucktail.
Tag: Oval gold.
Tail: Topping.
Hook: Sizes 2 to 10 single; 4 to 12 double low-water.

Wilkinson Shrimp
Body: First half, embossed silver tinsel; magenta cock middle hackle; rear half, embossed silver tinsel.
Throat: Kingfisher-blue dyed cock.
Cheeks: Jungle cock.
Head: Black varnish.
Tag: Oval gold.
Tail: Red golden pheasant flank feather.
Hook: Sizes 4 to 10 double low-water.

Silver Rat
Body: Flat silver ribbed with oval gold.
Wing: Badger hair (add grey squirrel in equal parts on small patterns).
Hackle: Grizzle cock or badger cock tied full circle.
Tag: Oval gold.
Tail: Topping.
Hook: Sizes 6 to 16 low-water double (Wilson).

Blue Charm
Body: Black floss ribbed with oval silver.
Wing: Bronze mallard with strips of teal along top and topping over all, ribbed with oval silver.
Hackle: Blue cock (dyed rich teal-blue shade).
Tag: Oval silver and yellow floss.
Tail: Topping.
Hook: Sizes 4 to 8 single; 10 double.

Curry's Shrimp

Body: Front half, red floss; badger cock middle hackle; black floss, rear half, ribbed with oval silver.
Wing: Two jungle cock feathers tied back to back.
Hackle: Badger cock.
Head: Red varnish.
Tag: Oval silver.
Tail: Red golden pheasant flank feather.
Hook: Sizes 6 to 8 low-water single or double.

Fox and Orange

Body: Black floss ribbed with flat silver tinsel.
Wing: Red guard hairs from fox's brush.
Hackle: Hot orange cock.
Tag: Flat silver.
Tail: Topping.
Hook: Sizes 6 to 8 single; 10 double

Dunkeld

Body: Flat gold ribbed with oval gold.
Wing: Bronze mallard over strips of red swan and topping over; jungle cock cheeks.
Hackle: Hot orange cock.
Throat: Blue jay or gallina dyed blue.
Tag: Oval silver and orange floss.
Butt: Black ostrich.
Tail: Topping and Indian crow substitute.
Hook: Sizes 6 to 10 single.

Stoat's Tail

Body: Black floss ribbed with flat silver.
Wing: Stoat's tail or squirrel dyed black.
Hackle: Black cock.
Tag: Oval silver.
Tail: Topping.
Hook: Sizes 4 to 8 single; 10 double

Blue Badger

Body: Black floss ribbed with oval silver.
Wing: Badger hair.
Hackle: Blue cock (teal-blue shade).
Tag: Oval silver and yellow floss.
Tail: Topping.
Hook: Sizes 4 to 8 single; 10 double

Connemara Black

Body: Black seal's fur ribbed with oval silver.
Wing: Bronze mallard over tippet in strands.
Hackle: Black cock with blue jay or gallina dyed blue in front.
Tag: Oval silver and orange floss.
Hook: Sizes 4 to 14 single.

SEA TROUT LURES

The Medicine

Body: Silver painted shank or silver tinsel.
Wing: Widgeon or brown mallard.
Tying silk: Red.
Hackle: Dyed bright-blue cock hackle.
Head: Red varnish.
Hook: Sizes 2 to 6 (low-water salmon hooks).

Sunk Lure

Tandem mount: 20 to 25lb (9–11kg) strength nylon, threaded through eyes of hooks and whipped to shank of both hooks; middle whipping on nylon between hooks. Overall length 2–3in (5–7.5cm). Apply two coats of varnish and coat with silver paint.
Wing: Two blue hackles, one either side, with a few strands of peacock herl on top. The wing should not extend beyond the point of the second hook.
Hook: Sizes 2 to 8.

SEA TROUT FLIES

Peter Ross

Body: Rear half, black silver tinsel; front half, red seal's fur; ribbed with oval silver.
Hackle: Black hen.
Wing: Barred teal flank feather.
Tail: Golden pheasant tippets.
Hook: Sizes: 8 to 14.

Watson's Fancy

Body: Rear half, red seal's fur; front half, black seal's fur, ribbed with oval silver.
Hackle: Black cock.

Wing: Crow quill fibres with small jungle cock either side.
Tail: Pheasant topping.
Hook: Sizes 8 to 14.

Keating's Killer
Body: Fiery brown seal's fur, ribbed with oval gold.
Hackle: Fiery brown cock.
Wing: Bronze mallard with small jungle cock either side.
Tail: Golden pheasant tippets.
Hook: Sizes 8 to 14.

Claret Bumble
Body: Medium claret seal's fur, ribbed with oval gold. Twin black and medium claret hackles palmered along body.
Hackle: Blue jay.
Tail: Golden pheasant tippets.
Hook: Sizes 8 to 14.

Black Pennell
Body: Black floss ribbed with oval silver.
Hackle: Black cock, tied full collar.
Tail: Golden pheasant tippets.
Hook: Sizes 8 to 14.

Daddy-Long-Legs
Body: Natural raffia ribbed with oval gold.
Legs: Six cock pheasant tail fibres knotted in the middle.
Hackle: Red game.
Wing: Two cree hackle tips.
Hook: Size 8.

Green Peter
Body: Four parts dark olive seal's fur with one part yellow seal's fur, ribbed with oval gold.
Wing: Slips of hen pheasant tail tied flat over body.
Hackle: Red cock hackle tied full collar.
Hook: Sizes 8 to 14.

Silver Doctor
Body: Flat silver, ribbed with oval silver.
Hackle: Kingfisher-blue cock.
Wing: Bronze mallard.
Head: Red varnish.

Tail: Topping
Butt: Red wool.
Hook: Sizes 8 to 14.

Delphi
Body: In two halves, rear half, flat silver tinsel ribbed oval silver; joined with black cock hackle to front half which is as rear half.
Hackle: Black cock.
Tail: Single jungle cock or double feathers tied back to back.
Hook: Sizes 8 to 12.

Duckfly (Daytime)
Body: Black floss.
Hackle: Black cock or hen.
Wing: Pair of white cock hackle tips.
Hook: Sizes 10 to 14.

Bloody Butcher
Body: Flat silver ribbed with oval silver.
Hackle: Scarlet cock.
Wing: Slips of blue mallard wing quills.
Hook: Sizes 8 to 12.

Bibio
Body: Three parts: black, hot orange, black seal's fur, ribbed with silver wire or oval silver.
Hackle: Black cock palmered with a second black cock hackle wound in front.
Hook: Sizes 8 to 14.

Kingsmill
Body: Black ostrich herl ribbed with oval gold or silver wire.
Hackle: Black cock.
Wing: Slips of crow quill tied low over body; topping over.
Cheeks: Jungle cock.
Tag: Blue floss.
Tail: Topping.
Hook: Sizes 8 to 14

BROWN TROUT FLIES

River

Mayfly Dun (*Ephemera danica*)
Body: Mixture of hare's ear and yellow seal's fur, ribbed with gold wire.
Hackle: At shoulder only, tied half-circle; a long-fibred green-grey, olive cock's hackle, with a few turns of a shorter-fibred light yellow cock's hackle run through it.
Tails: Three fibres of pheasant tail.
Hook: Sizes 8 to 10.

Mayfly Spinner (Spent Gnat) — Female
Body: Natural white raffia, ribbed gold wire, and ribbed with short-fibred badger cock hackle.
Hackle: Blue dun, or cream cock's hackle dyed blue grey, tied spent.
Tails: Three fibres of pheasant tail.
Hook: Sizes 8 to 10.

Mayfly Nymph
Body: Primrose seal's fur with dark hare's ear, fur laid along back and held down by ribbing of narrow gold tinsel. On front half of body, hare's ear fur is picked out between the ribbing, to suggest dorsal gills of nymph.
Wing cases: Brown feather with pale markings (eg from a pheasant or a turkey) tied in the conventional nymph fashion.
Hackle: Soft greyish hen hackles dyed yellow.
Tails: Fibres of pale-greyish mallard flank feathers dyed yellow.
Hook: Sizes 8 to 10.

Cinnamon Sedge (*Limnephilus* spp.)
Body: Black fibre from a turkey tail, rook's wing or the like, used as herl, ribbed gold wire.
Wing: Rook or jackdaw wing feather.
Hackle: Throat only — coch-y-bonddhu cock.
Hook: Sizes 8 to 10.

Iron Blue Dun (*Baetis pumilus*)
Body: Dull slate-purple tying silk varnished.

Hackle: Cream cock, dyed gunmetal, full circle.
Tails: As hackle.
Hook: Sizes 14 to 16.

Hare's Ear (*Baetis* spp.)
Body: Dark fur from the base of a hare's ear spun on yellow tying silk.
Rib: Flat gold tinsel.
Hackle: Rusty blue dun cock or hen or, in spring, a dark-olive hackle.
Tail: Three long body strands or three dark olive fibres.
Hook: Sizes 12 to 16.

Greenwell's Glory (*Baetis* spp.)
Body: Olive tying silk, ribbed gold wire.
Hackle: Coch-y-bonddhu cock (brown, with dark centre and tips), tied full circle.
Tails: Three fibres of coch-y-bonddhu cock.
Hook: Sizes 12 to 16.

Orange Quill (*Ephemerella ignita*)
Body: Peacock quill died hot orange.
Hackle: Blue dun cock, or white cock, dyed deep blue-grey, full circle.
Tails: Brown cock.
Hook: Size 14.

Female B.W.O. (*Ephemerella ignita*)
Body: Olive tying silk, ribbed gold wire; or olive tying silk lightly dubbed with yellow olive seal's fur, ribbed gold wire.
Hackle: Blue-grey, full circle, with light yellowish- olive wound behind it.
Tails: Ginger cock.
Hook: Size 14.

Lunn's Particular (*Baetis* spp.)
Body: Deep-orange floss or hackle-stalk dyed orange, ribbed with gold wire on floss-bodied version only.
Wing: Pale blue dun hackle points dyed spent.
Hackle: Rhode Island Red cock.
Silk: Pale orange.
Tail: Light ginger cock fibres.
Hook: Sizes 14 to 16.

Spent Olive (*Baetis* spp.)
Body: Crimson tying silk, lightly and thinly dubbed with claret seal's fur, ribbed gold wire.
Hackle: Blue dun, or cream cock dyed pale blue-grey, tied spent.
Tails: Blue-grey or brown cock.
Hook: Sizes 12 to 14.

Sawyer Nymph (*Baetis* spp.)
Underbody: Copper wire with a hump for a thorax.
Overbody: Pheasant tail fibres wound on with the copper wire and tied fatter at the thorax.
Wingcase: Pheasant tail fibres doubled and redoubled.
Tail: Three cock-pheasant tail fibres.
Hook: Sizes 12 to 18.

Tup's Indispensable (*Baetis* spp.)
Body: Primrose tying silk, lightly dubbed towards the thorax with mixture of pale pink and primrose seal's fur or sheep's wool; ribbed with gold wire.
Hackle: Palest honey dun, full circle.
Tails: Honey dun.
Hook: Sizes 14 to 16.

Lake

Invicta
Body: Dull yellow seal's fur, ribbed silver tinsel.
Wing: Woodcock.
Hackle: Hen dyed pale yellow-olive, mixed with fibres of jay's wing.
Tails: Golden pheasant tippet.
Hook: Sizes 8 to 10.

Black and Peacock Spider
Body: Peacock herl, short and fat, with a protective but concealed rib of gold wire.
Hackle: A few turns only of long, soft black hen or young cock hackle. Bring body close up behind hackle, so that hackle stands out at right angles to the hook so that pressure of water, when fly is 'worked', forces fibres back.
Hook: Sizes 8 to 12.

Claret and Mallard
Body: Claret seal's fur.
Rib: Fine gold tinsel or wire.
Hackle: Natural light hen.
Wing: Brown mallard.
Tail: Golden pheasant tippets.
Hook: Sizes 8 to 12.

Green Peter (*Phryganea varia*)
Body: Green seal's fur, ribbed gold wire.
Wing: Speckled ginger or red brown hen.
Hackle: Throat only — light red cock.
Hook: Sizes 6 to 10.

Wickham's Fancy
Body: Flat gold tinsel.
Body hackle: Palmered ginger-red cock, ribbed gold wire.
Wing: Medium starling wings set upright and split for the floating dressing, or across the back for wet-fly version.
Tail: Guinea-fowl dyed reddish-brown, or ginger hackles.
Hook: Sizes 8 to 12.

Golden Olive
Body: Yellow seal's fur, mixed with hare's ear, ribbed gold wire.
Wing: Starling primary.
Hackle: Hen dyed yellow-olive.
Tails: Golden pheasant tippet; or cock hackle black fibre dyed yellow-olive.
Hook: Sizes 8 to 12.

Murrough (*Phryganea* spp.)
Body: Red-brown seal's fur, ribbed gold wire.
Wing: Red-brown, black-speckled feathers from hen's wing.
Hackle: (Throat) Rhode Island Red cock; (rib) coch-y-bonddhu cock.
Hook: Sizes 8 to 10.

Green Peter (pupa)
Body: Green seal's fur, slip of dark green olive feather, gold tinsel rib.

Wing: Dark speckled grey pheasant wing.
Legs: Mallard scapular fibres and/or a few turns of ginger hen.
Hook: Sizes 6 to 10.

Murrough (pupa)
Body: Orange seal's fur, mixed with some hare's ear, slip of dark brown feather, golden tinsel rib.
Wing: Speckled ginger or speckled light brown hen.
Legs: Mallard scapular fibres mixed with some ginger hen.
Hook: Sizes 6 to 10.

RAINBOW TROUT LURES

Scarlet and Mallard
Body: Scarlet seal's fur.
Rib: Fine gold tinsel or wire.
Hackle: Natural light hen.
Wing: Brown mallard.
Tail: Golden pheasant tippets.
Hook: Sizes 8 to 12.

Baby Doll
Body, Back and Tail: White nylon Sirdar baby wool.
Head: Black tying silk.
Hook: Sizes 6 to 8 (long shank).

Black Chenille
Body: Black chenille, ribbed medium silver tinsel.
Wings: Four black hackles of equal length extending beyond the hook.
Beard hackle: Black hackle fibres.
Tail: Black hackle fibres or hackle tip.
Hook: Sizes 6 to 8 (long shank).

Badger Matuka
Body: Fluorescent-orange wool, ribbed with fine oval silver tinsel.
Wing: Two badger cock hackles in matuka style, two jungle-cock eye cheeks.
Beard hackle: Hot-orange or scarlet cock.
Hook: Sizes 6 to 8 (long shank).

Whiskey Fly
Body: Flat silver or gold Mylar or Lurex with a butt of scarlet or red fluorescent floss, ribbed with scarlet or red fluorescent floss, whole body is then clear varnished.
Wing: Hot-orange calf tail tied as long as the body.
Hook: Sizes 6 to 10 (long shank).

Stickfly
Body: Dark cock-pheasant tail fibres and few olive swan herls wound together over a varnished shank, ribbed with copper, silver or gold tinsel, on their own or in combination, wound the opposite way to the body herls and ribbed with green peacock herl.
Thorax: Yellow or off-white floss silk.
Hackle: Sparsely-tied pale ginger cock.
Head: Varnished black or dark-olive tying silk.
Hook: Sizes 8 to 10 (long shank).

Appetiser
Body: White chenille, ribbed fine oval silver tinsel.
Wing: A generous spray of white marabou herl overlaid with a bunch of natural grey squirrel hair.
Beard hackle: A mixture of dark green and orange hackle fibres with silver mallard breast feathers.
Tail: Mixed dark-green and orange cock hackle fibres and silver mallard breast-feathers.
Head: Black tying silk.
Hook: Size 6 (long shank).

Muddler Minnow
Body: Flat gold tinsel.
Wing: Grey squirrel fibres between two matched mottled oak-turkey wing sections.
Head: Deer hair spun and clipped to a ball shape, leaving a few long fibres trailing to the rear as a hackle.
Tail: A folded slip of oak-turkey wing feather.
Hook: Sizes 4 to 12 (long shank).

APPENDIX 2

Useful addresses

Central Fisheries Board
Balnagowan
Mobhi Boreen
Glasnevin
Dublin 9
Tel: (01) 379206

Bord Fáilte/Irish Tourist Board
Baggot Street Bridge
Dublin 2
Tel: (01) 765871

Department of Agriculture for Northern Ireland
Fisheries Division
Hut 5 Castle Grounds
Stormont
Belfast BT4 3TA
Tel: Belfast 63939

Foyle Fisheries Commission
8 Victoria Road
Derry BT47 2AB
Tel: (0504) 42100

Northern Ireland Tourist Board
River House
48 High Street
Belfast BT1 2DS
Tel: Belfast 31221

Shannon Regional Fisheries Board
Thomond Weir
Limerick
Tel: (061) 55171

South Western Regional Fisheries Board
1 Nevilles Terrace
Massey Town
Macroom
Co. Cork
Tel: (026) 41221

Southern Regional Fisheries Board
Anglesea Street
Clonmel
Co. Tipperary
Tel: (052) 23624

Eastern Regional Fisheries Board
Mobhi Boreen
Glasnevin
Dublin 9
Tel: (01) 379206

Northern Regional Fisheries Board
Station Road
Ballyshannon
Co. Donegal
Tel: (072) 51435

North Western Regional Fisheries Board
Abbey Street
Ballina
Co. Mayo
Tel: (096) 22788

Western Regional Fisheries Board
Weir Lodge
Earl's Island
Galway
Tel: (091) 63118/119/110

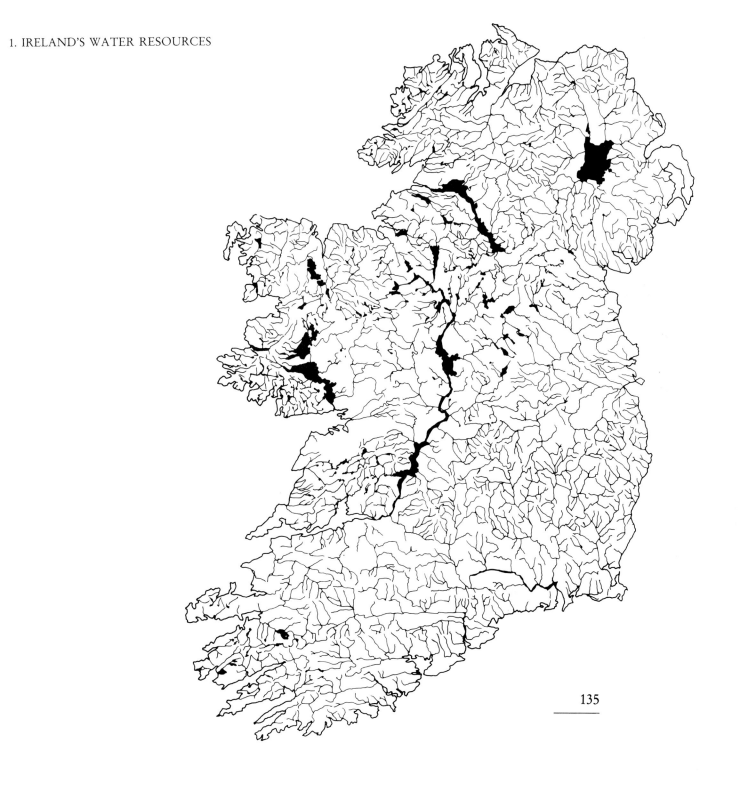

135

1. R. Liffey
2. R. Slaney
3. R. Blackwater
4. R. Lee
5. L. Currane System
6. R. Caragh Upr
7. R. Laune & L. Leane
8. R. Feale
9. R. Shannon
10. R Corrib & L. Corrib
11. R. Ballynahinch &
    L. Inagh/Derryclare
12. Erriff System
13. Delphi System
14. L. Beltra & Newport River
15. R. Owenduff
16. R. Moy & L. Conn
17. L. Gill & Garavogue River
18. R. Bundrowse & L. Melvin
19. R. Lackagh
20. R. Foyle & tributaries
21. R. Fane
22. R. Dee
23. R. Boyne & tributaries

3. GRILSE FISHERIES

1. R. Liffey
2. R. Blackwater
3. R. Lee
4. R. Bandon
5. R. Sheen
6. L. Currane
7. R. Inny
8. Caragh System
9. R. Laune & Killarney Lakes
10. R. Feale
11. R. Mulcair
12. R. Shannon
13. R. Corrib & L. Corrib
14. Screebe Fishery
15. Ballynahinch Fishery
16. Kylemore Fishery
17. Erriff Fishery
18. Delphi Fishery
19. Newport Fishery
20. Burrishoole Fishery
21. Owenduff Fishery
22. Owenmore Fishery
23. R. Moy & L. Conn
24. R. Easkey
25. Ballisodare Fishery
26. Glencar Lake
27. R. Bundrowse & L. Melvin
28. R. Owenea
29. L. Lackagh
30. R. Crana
31. R. Foyle & tributaries
32. R. Bann
33. R. Bush
34. R. Fane
35. R. Boyne

137

Brown trout fisheries

1. R. Liffey
2. R. Suir
3. R. Awbeg
4. R. Funcheon
5. R. Laune & L. Leane
6. L. Ree
7. L. Derg
8. L. Glore
9. L. Lene
10. R. Bunowen
11. R. Shiven
12. R. Killeglan
13. R. Brosna & tributaries
14. L. Owel
15. L. Ennell
16. R. Little Brosna
17. R Maigue & tributaries
18. R. Fergus
19. L. Inchiquin
20. R. Kilcolgan
21. L. Rea
22. L. Corrib
23. L. Mask
24. L. Carra
25. L. Conn/L. Cullen
26. R. Unshin
27. L. Arrow
28. L. Melvin
29. L. Erne Lwr
30. R. Boyne & tributaries

Managed (stocked) fisheries
(Brown (B) and rainbow (R) trout)

31. Blessington Resv. (B)
32. Waterford Resv. (R & B)
33. L. Aderry (R)
34. L. Garranes (R)
35. Shepperton Lakes (R)
36. L. Driminidy (R)
37. Schull Resv. (R)
38. L. Bofinne (R)
39. L. Avaul (R)
40. L. Fada (R)
41. L. Barfinnihy (R)
42. L. na Kirka (R)
43. L. O'Flynn (B)
44. Mount Dalton Lake (B)
45. L. Acalla (R)
46. Pallas Lake (R)
47. Castlebar Lakes (B)
48. L. Bo (R) and L. na Léibe (R)
49. Moyduff Lake (R)
50. Annagh Lake (R)
51. Mill (R & B)
52. Coolyermer L. (B)
53. L. Keenaghan (R & B)
54. L. Bradan (B)
55. L. Brantry (B)
56. L. Moor/L. Ash (B)
57. Altnahinch Resv. (B)
58. Dungonnell Resv. (B)
59. Killylane Resv. (B)
60. Woodburn Resv. (R & B)
61. Stonyford & Leathemstown Resv. (R & B)
62. Portavoe Resv. (R & B)
63. Hillsborough L. (R & B)
64. Craigavon City Parks (R)
65. Ballykeel Lougherne (R & B)
66. L. Brickland (R & B)
67. Castlewellan L. (R & B)
68. Spelga Resv. (R & B)
69. Emy L. (B)
70. White L. (R)

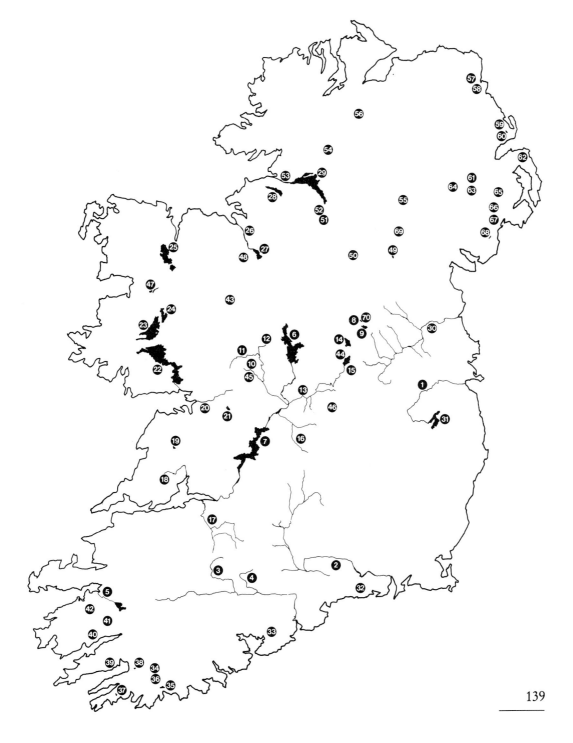

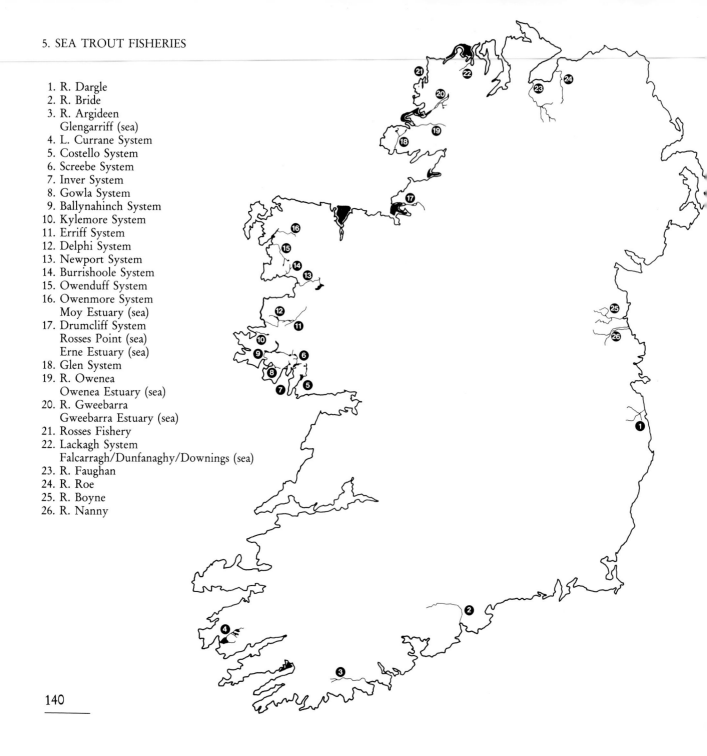

1. R. Dargle
2. R. Bride
3. R. Argideen
   Glengarriff (sea)
4. L. Currane System
5. Costello System
6. Screebe System
7. Inver System
8. Gowla System
9. Ballynahinch System
10. Kylemore System
11. Erriff System
12. Delphi System
13. Newport System
14. Burrishoole System
15. Owenduff System
16. Owenmore System
    Moy Estuary (sea)
17. Drumcliff System
    Rosses Point (sea)
    Erne Estuary (sea)
18. Glen System
19. R. Owenea
    Owenea Estuary (sea)
20. R. Gweebarra
    Gweebarra Estuary (sea)
21. Rosses Fishery
22. Lackagh System
    Falcarragh/Dunfanaghy/Downings (sea)
23. R. Faughan
24. R. Roe
25. R. Boyne
26. R. Nanny

BIBLIOGRAPHY

Angling Guide — Department of Agriculture for Northern Ireland. 108pp

The Angler's Guide — Department of Agriculture, Fisheries Branch, Dublin. (1948) The Stationery Office. 261pp

Annual Reports of the Inland Fisheries Trust. (1951-80) IFT, Glasnevin, Dublin.

The Biology of the Sea Trout. Summary of a symposium held at Plas Menai, Wales, 24-26 October 1984. Atlantic Salmon Trust, Pitlochry, Scotland. 42pp

CHURCH, B. (1977) *Reservoir Trout Fishing.* (Modern Angling Series) Cassell and Co. Ltd, London. 1st. edn. 136pp

CHURCH, B. and GATHERCOLE, P. (1985) *Imitations of the Trout's World.* The Crowood Press, Crowood Hse, Ramsbury, Marlborough, Wiltshire. 154pp

de BUITLEAR, ÉAMON (ed.) (1985) *Irish Rivers.* Country House, Dublin. 128pp

FAHY, E. (1985) *Child of the Tides.* The Glendale Press, Dublin. 188pp

FALKUS, H. (1984) *Salmon Fishing.* H. F. and G. Witherby Ltd, London. 448pp

(1986) *Sea Trout Fishing.* H. F. and G. Witherby Ltd, London. 448pp

FALLON, NIALL (1983) *Fly Fishing for Irish trout.* Roberts Books, Kilkenny, Ireland. 146pp

FROST, W. E. (1975) 'A survey of the rainbow trout (*Salmo gairdneri* L.) in Britain and Ireland.' Freshwater Biological Association, Windermere, England. 35pp

HARRIS, G. and MORGAN, M. (1989) *Successful Sea Trout Angling — The Practical Guide.* Blandford Press, London. 400pp

Inland Fisheries — Strategies for Management and Development. (1986) Central Fisheries Board, Dublin. 199pp

Ireland — Brown Trout Fishing. (1965) Bord Fáilte Éireann, Dublin. 125pp

Irish Sport Fishes — A Guide to their Identification. Central Fisheries Board, Dublin. 66pp

KENNEDY, M. and FITZMAURICE, P. (1971) 'Growth and food of brown trout (*Salmo trutta* L.) in Irish waters.' Proc. RIA, vol. 71, sect. B, no. 18, 269-352

KENNEDY, M. (1972) *Trout flies for Irish waters.* The Inland Fisheries Trust Inc, Dublin. 42pp

KINGSMILL-MOORE, T.C. (1960) *A Man May Fish.* Herbert Jenkins, London. 1st edn. 192pp

MacCRIMMON, H. R. (1971) 'World distribution of rainbow trout (*Salmo gairdneri*).' *J. Fish. Res. Board Can.,* 28:663-704

MILLS, D.H. and HADOKE, G.D.F. (1986) *Atlantic Salmon Facts.* The Atlantic Salmon Trust, Moulin, Pitlochry, Scotland. 24pp

OGLESBY, A. (1983) *Salmon.* Queen Ann Press, London. 255pp

O'REILLY, P. (1987) *Trout and Salmon Loughs of Ireland — A Fisherman's Guide.* Unwin Hyman, London. 299pp

WHELAN, K.F. (1979) 'Some aspects of the biology of *Ephemera danica* mull (Ephemerida: Ephemeroptera) in Irish waters.' (187-200) in *Advances in Ephemeroptera Biology.* J.F. Flannagan and K.E. Marshall (eds.). Plenum Press, New York. 187-200pp

INDEX